VGM's
HANDBOOK
of BUSINESS
&
MANAGEMENT
CAREERS

edited by Annette Selden

VGM Career Horizons
a division of *NTC Publishing Group*
Lincolnwood, Illinois USA

Library of Congress Cataloging-in-Publication Data

VGM's handbook of business & management careers / edited by Annette Selden.
    p. cm.

  ISBN 0-8442-4140-7 (paper)

   1. Business—Vocational guidance—United States. 2. Management—
Vocational guidance—United States. I. Selden, Annette. II. VGM
Career Horizons (Firm) III. Title: VGM's handbook of business and
management careers.
HF5382.5.U5V48 1993
650'.023'73—dc20   92-41818
                                                           CIP

Published by VGM Career Horizons, a division of NTC Publishing Group.
© 1993 by NTC Publishing Group, 4255 West Touhy Avenue,
Lincolnwood (Chicago), Illinois 60646-1975 U.S.A.
All rights reserved. No part of this book may be reproduced, stored
in a retrieval system, or transmitted in any form or by any means,
electronic, mechanical, photocopying, recording or otherwise, without
the prior permission of NTC Publishing Group.
Manufactured in the United States of America.

3 4 5 6 7 8 9 0 VP 9 8 7 6 5 4 3 2 1

Contents

Contents

Accountant

The Job   Accountants prepare and analyze the financial reports that furnish up-to-date information for businesses, government agencies, and other organizations. The data they provide influence just about every business and government decision, since the financial condition of an organization is an ever-present ingredient of any decision. There are also many opportunities for part-time work, especially with small businesses.

There are three major accounting fields: public, management, and government. Some accountants are *public accountants* who work for a number of clients; they work for themselves or for an accounting firm. Public accountants often specialize in one phase of accounting, such as auditing or taxes. Many also function as management consultants, advising clients on accounting systems and equipment.

Certified public accountants (CPAs) must hold a certificate issued by the state board of accountancy. To obtain certification they usually must have a college degree and pass the CPA examination prepared by the American Institute of Certified Public Accountants. Seventeen states now require 150 semester hours of college course work. These hours are usually acquired in a four-year bachelor's-degree or master's-degree program.

Other accountants are management accountants, employed by a single company to handle the company's financial records.

Some management accountants function as internal *auditors*. Auditing entails reviewing financial records and reports to judge their reliability. The internal auditor's evaluation of the financial systems and management control procedures of a company enables the company to function efficiently and economically.

In some companies a management accountant may function as a credit manager, handling the company's accounts receivable and making decisions on extending credit to customers.

Government accountants maintain and examine the financial records of government agencies and audit the records of businesses and individuals whose financial activities are subject to government regulations.

Beginners in accounting usually start as ledger accountants, junior internal auditors, or as trainees for technical accounting positions. Junior public accountants usually assist with auditing work for several clients.

Related jobs are credit manager, FBI special agent, and internal revenue agent.

1

Places of Employment and Working Conditions   All business, industrial, and government organizations use the services of accountants. Accountants work for the corner deli operator as well as for AT&T; for the smallest municipal government as well as for the government of the United States. They work throughout the country, with the heaviest concentration of job opportunities in large urban areas where many public accounting firms and central offices of large businesses are located.

Accountants have desk jobs and generally work between 35 and 40 hours a week. Those employed by accounting firms carry heavy work loads during tax season, roughly from early December to May. Accountants employed by national firms may travel extensively to conduct audits and perform other services for their clients or employers.

Qualifications, Education, and Training   If you want to be an accountant, you need an aptitude for mathematics. In addition, you must be neat, accurate, able to work with little supervision, and able to handle responsibility.

Training in accounting is available at business schools and correspondence schools, as well as at colleges and universities. However, most large public accounting and business firms require beginning accountants and internal auditors to have at least a bachelor's degree in accounting or in a closely related field. Many employers prefer a master's degree. Many companies also require familiarity with computer technology. The federal government requires a bachelor's degree with at least 24 semester hours of accounting or an equivalent combination of college and work experience.

Work experience is important and can help an applicant get a job after graduation. Therefore, many colleges provide students with an opportunity to gain experience through internship programs while still in school.

Accountants who wish to advance professionally must continue studying accounting throughout their careers. Seminars and courses are offered by many employers and professional associations. More and more accountants are studying computer operation and programming in addition to accounting subjects.

In the field of internal auditing, the designation *certified internal auditor* (CIA) is awarded by The Institute of Internal Auditors to those who have two years' experience and complete a four-part examination. Candidates for this designation must also have a bachelor's degree from an accredited college or university.

In the majority of states, CPAs are the only accountants who are licensed or regulated; most states require CPA candidates to be college graduates, while a few accept a certain number of years of experience in lieu of a college degree.

More and more states are requiring both CPAs and licensed public accountants to complete continuing education courses for license renewal.

Potential and Advancement
There are about 985,000 accountants in the United States; about 40 percent are CPAs and 17 percent are CIAs. The demand for skilled accountants is expected to increase rapidly through the year 2005 as business and government agencies continue to grow in size and complexity.

There will be ample job opportunities for accountants with college degrees and a broad background of education and experience. In large companies, when it comes to promotions, accountants who lack academic credentials may find themselves lagging behind those with advanced degrees.

Accountants may advance to such jobs as chief plant accountant, chief cost accountant, budget director, or manager of internal auditing. Some achieve corporate-level positions such as controller, treasurer, financial vice president, or president.

Public accountants can advance from beginner through intermediate-level positions to senior positions in about five years, as they gain experience and handle more complex accounts. In large accounting firms, they often become supervisors, managers, or partners. Some transfer to executive positions in private firms or open their own public accounting offices.

Income
Salaries for beginning public accountants employed by public accounting firms average $25,300 a year. Salaries of management accountants in private industry average $24,700 a year. Some of the most experienced management accountants earn up to $80,000 annually. Experienced internal auditors average salaries of $36,800 a year.

Chief accountants who direct the accounting program of a company earn from $43,000 to over $74,000, depending on the size of the accounting staff and the scope of authority.

In the federal government, salaries for all accountants average around $40,000 a year. Junior accountants and auditors begin at about $17,000; those with superior academic records can begin as high as $21,000. A beginner with a master's degree or two years of professional experience starts at $25,700.

Additional Sources of Information

American Institute of Certified Public Accountants
1211 Avenue of the Americas
New York, NY 10036

National Society of Public Accountants
1010 North Fairfax Street
Alexandria, VA 22314

The Institute of Internal Auditors
249 Maitland Avenue
Altamonte Springs, FL 32701

Actuary

The Job   Actuaries are, for the most part, mathematicians. They assemble and analyze statistics on probabilities of death, illness, injury, disability, unemployment, retirement, and property losses to design insurance and pension plans and set up the premium structure for the policies.

For example, statistics on auto accidents are gathered and analyzed by actuaries employed by a company selling auto insurance. The actuaries then base the premiums for their company's policies on the accident statistics for different groups of policyholders. They consider age, miles driven annually, and geographic location, among other things.

Since the insurance company is assuming a risk, the premium rates developed by company actuaries must enable the company to pay all claims and expenses and must be adequate to provide the company with a reasonable profit for assuming that risk. To function effectively, actuaries must keep up-to-date on general economic and social trends and on any legislative developments that might affect insurance practices.

Actuaries provide information to executives in their company's investments, group underwriting, and pension planning departments; they prepare material for policyholders and government requirements; and they may be called on to testify before public agencies regarding proposed legislation on insurance practices.

Actuaries employed by the federal government usually work on a specific insurance or pension program such as Social Security. Those in state government positions regulate insurance companies, supervise state pension programs, and work in the unemployment insurance and workers' compensation programs.

Consulting actuaries set up pension and welfare plans for private companies, unions, and government agencies. Some consulting actuaries evaluate pension plans and certify their solvency in compliance with the Employee Retirement Income Security Act of 1974.

Private insurance companies employ over one-half of all actuaries, with life insurance companies employing the most. Large companies may employ over 100 actuaries; many smaller companies use the services of consulting firms or rating bureaus. Other actuaries work for private organizations that administer independent pension or welfare plans, or for federal and state agencies.

Beginning actuaries often rotate among various jobs within a company's actuarial operation to become familiar with its different phases. In the process, they gain a broad knowledge of insurance and related fields.

Related jobs are mathematician, statistician, and underwriter.

Places of Employment and Working Conditions

Many actuaries work in Boston, Chicago, Hartford, New York City, Philadelphia and Des Moines.

Actuaries have desk jobs and usually work at least a 40-hour week. Occasional overtime is necessary.

Qualifications, Education, and Training

A strong background in mathematics is necessary for anyone interested in a career as an actuary.

Only 38 colleges and universities offer a degree in actuarial science. However, a bachelor's degree with a major in mathematics, statistics, or business administration is also a good educational background for an actuary. Courses in insurance law, economics, and accounting are valuable.

Of equal importance to a strong mathematics background are the examination programs offered by professional actuarial societies to prospective actuaries. Examinations are given twice a year, and extensive home study is required to pass the more advanced ones. Completion of one or more of these examinations while still in school helps students to evaluate their potential as actuaries; those who pass one or more examinations usually have better employment opportunities and receive higher starting salaries. Actuaries are encouraged to complete an entire series of examinations as early as possible in their careers to achieve full professional status. This usually takes from five to ten years.

Associate membership in their respective professional societies is awarded to actuaries after successful completion of half the examinations in the life insurance or pension series, or seven examinations in the casualty series. Full membership is awarded, along with the title "fellow," upon completion of an entire series.

Consulting pension actuaries who service private pension plans and certify the plans' solvency must be enrolled and licensed by the Joint Board for the Enrollment of Actuaries, which stipulates the experience and education required.

Potential and Advancement

There are about 13,000 persons employed as actuaries in the United States. Employment in this field is expected to grow rapidly through the year 2005, with job opportunities best for college graduates who have passed at least two actuarial examinations while still in school. Even though the field is expected to have substantial growth, the large number of new graduates with degrees in actuarial science, mathematics, and statistics will mean increased competition for available job openings.

Advancement within the field depends on job performance, experience, and the number of actuarial examinations successfully completed. Actuaries can be promoted to assistant, associate, and chief actuary within their company. Because they have a broad knowledge of insurance and its related fields, actuaries are often selected for administrative positions in other company departments such as underwriting, accounting, or data processing. Many actuaries advance to top executive positions, where they help determine company policy.

Income   Recent college graduates just beginning their careers earn, on average, about $28,300 a year, and slightly less if they have not passed any actuarial examinations. Earnings increase with experience and advancement in the examination program with many companies giving merit increases and cash bonuses for each examination successfully completed.

Once membership in a professional society is achieved, associate members average about $43,100 annually; those awarded full fellowships average about $61,900.

Additional Sources of Information

American Society of Pension Actuaries
2029 K Street, NW
4th Floor
Washington, DC 20006

Casualty Actuarial Society
1100 North Glebe Road
Suite 600
Arlington, VA 22201

Society of Actuaries
475 North Martingale Road
Suite 800
Schaumburg, IL 60173

Advertising Account Executive

The Job Each of an advertising agency's clients is assigned to an account executive who is responsible for handling everything related to the client's advertising campaign. The account executive must know the client's product and marketing plans and the agency's resources for successfully carrying out the client's requirements. The account executive plans the advertising campaign and creates its components.

The account executive studies a client's company and its sales, its present public image, and its advertising requirements and budget. In developing an advertising campaign to suit the client's needs, the account executive calls upon all the resources of the agency's artists and designers, copywriters, media buyers, production staff, and market researchers.

The account executive then has the job of selling the client on the planned advertising campaign. Considerable time may be spent changing and reworking the plan before the client grants approval. As the advertising campaign progresses, the account executive keeps track of sales figures and may further alter the campaign to achieve the results the client wants.

The job of account executives can sometimes be glamorous—they get to wine and dine the clients and sometimes go on location to oversee the production of commercials or other material for a client—but it also carries a great deal of responsibility. The account executive must ensure that artists, copywriters, and production people meet schedules, and must act as liaison between the agency and the client, keeping costs within the client's budget.

In some large agencies, account executives report to an *account supervisor,* but in most agencies they are supervised by top management or owners of the agency. In small agencies, the owners of the firm often function as account executives and may even do some of the creative work, such as copywriting.

Places of Employment and Working Conditions Advertising agencies exist in many cities, but the heaviest concentrations are in New York City, Los Angeles, and Chicago. "Madison Avenue" is, of course, the term applied to the many large and prestigious agencies in New York City. Other rapidly growing advertising centers are Atlanta, Houston, Dallas, and Detroit.

Pressures are extreme and working hours are long and unpredictable. Advertising is a very competitive field, and there is very little job security. The loss of a large account can mean the firing or the laying off of everyone who worked on the account, including the account executive.

Qualifications, Education, and Training
Job experience in sales, advertising, or market research is valuable, but you also need at least a bachelor's degree to become an advertising account executive. A major in advertising, marketing, business administration, or liberal arts is preferred, and some large agencies prefer a master's degree in business administration.

Training programs for account executives are offered by some agencies.

Potential and Advancement
The employment outlook for the advertising field is good, and job opportunities should continue to grow through the year 2005. The advertising field is strongly affected by general business conditions, however, since most firms expand or contract their advertising budgets according to how their own sales are affected by economic conditions. Entry-level jobs and trainee positions usually have an overabundance of applicants, but experienced account executives with a proven track record will continue to be in demand.

Skilled and experienced account executives can advance to the highest positions in an agency. In a large agency, they can become account supervisors of one or more accounts, advance to the executive suite, become partners in the firm, or open their own agencies. Some leave their agency jobs to become advertising managers for former clients.

Income
Trainees start at around $20,000 to $31,000 a year, depending on education and the size of the agency. Account supervisors average between $41,500 and $51,900, again, depending on the size of the agency. Account executives average from $30,100 in smaller agencies to $36,100 or higher in large agencies.

Additional Sources of Information

American Advertising Federation
1400 K Street, NW
Suite 1000
Washington, DC 20005

Business/Professional Advertising Association
100 Metroplex Drive
Edison, NJ 08817

American Association of Advertising Agencies
666 Third Avenue
13th Floor
New York, NY 10017

Advertising Manager

The Job In many companies the amount of advertising done to place the company's product or service before the public requires the time and talents of a full-time advertising manager. Working in close cooperation with the marketing department or as part of the marketing department, the advertising manager develops advertising appropriate to the consumers the company wants to attract.

In some companies the advertising manager is the only one on the staff, creating art and written copy and placing it in newspapers, magazines, and radio or television as well. Other advertising managers supervise a staff that may include artists, copywriters, production and research workers, and media buyers. The department may turn out display ads, point-of-sale and direct mail advertising, a company product catalog, and trade show displays. In such advertising departments, the advertising manager is responsible for the administration of a large budget, coordinates the activities of the department to meet deadlines and schedules, places the company's advertising in the appropriate media vehicles, and handles the day-to-day administration of the department.

In a company that uses the services of an advertising agency for all or part of its advertising, the advertising manager represents the company in its dealings with the agency. Depending on the extent of the manager's authority, he or she might select the advertising agency, supervise the handling of the account by the agency, supply market research information, apportion the advertising budget, and approve the final advertising campaign. In some companies, top management has the final approval of the advertising campaign and budget.

Regardless of whether the advertising manager works with an advertising agency or supervises an in-house advertising department, and regardless of the size of the company or the budget it allows for advertising, the advertising manager is expected to produce visible results in the form of increased sales volume of the company's product or service.

Places of Employment and Working Conditions   Advertising managers work in all areas of the country, with the most job opportunities in large metropolitan areas.

Advertising managers work under considerable pressure. They generally work long hours and are required to coordinate successfully the ideas, personalities, and talents of a variety of people—from top management to the creative staff of the advertising department.

Qualifications, Education, and Training
Success in advertising depends on imagination, creativity, a knowledge of what motivates consumers, and the ability to function as part of a team. An advertising manager must also have supervisory ability, budgeting experience, and a solid grounding in all areas of advertising.

The first step is a must—a college degree. The most useful degrees are liberal arts, business administration, or marketing.

After graduation, beginners in this field usually start in one of the specialty areas of advertising such as art, copywriting, research, production, or media buying in either an advertising department or advertising agency to gain as much experience as possible. Experience in several different specialties provides the best training for a prospective advertising manager.

Potential and Advancement
As with all top management positions, there is competition for the top spot in an advertising department. The job outlook is good for the future because of the high level of domestic and foreign competition in products and services. The best jobs will go to those with education, experience, and proven abilities in advertising.

Advertising managers are already in top positions. They advance by moving to larger companies or to advertising agencies where they will have greater responsibilities and more challenging work. Some open their own advertising agencies.

Income
Salaries vary from $20,300 to $78,500, depending on location, sales volume, and size of company. In general, salaries for advertising managers are higher in manufacturing firms than in nonmanufacturing firms.

Many advertising managers also receive bonuses or company stock for effective advertising campaigns and participate in profit-sharing plans.

Additional Sources of Information

American Advertising Federation
1400 K Street, NW
Suite 1000
Washington, DC 20005

Association of National Advertisers
155 East 44th Street
New York, NY 10017

Business/Professional Advertising Association
100 Metroplex Drive
Edison, NJ 08817

American Association of Advertising Agencies
666 Third Avenue
13th Floor
New York, NY 10017

Advertising Sales Person

The Job The money necessary to finance the activities of radio and television stations and most of the publication costs of newspapers and magazines comes from the sale of time or space to clients who wish to advertise a product or service.

Advertising sales people sell directly to clients or to advertising agencies that represent the clients. Technically, the sales worker is selling broadcasting time segments on the stations or space in the publications, but actually what is being sold is the station's programming or a publication's content and the amount and type of audience that each attracts.

Newspapers get a portion of the dollars spent on advertising. Advertising sales people in this field work both locally and as *national sales representatives*. There are three principal categories of newspaper advertising: general, retail, and classified. General, also known as national, advertising is the advertising of products and services marketed nationally or regionally through local retail outlets. This type of newspaper advertising is usually handled by independent national sales representatives who deal with national advertisers and their advertising agencies. They usually represent a number of local newspapers.

Retail advertising is local advertising. Sales people handling this type of newspaper advertising may also provide some of the copywriting and layout required or provide advice on an ad content and design. Classified advertising is sold by outside sales persons who call on auto dealers, real estate brokers, and other regular advertisers and by inside sales people who handle walk-in or telephone classified advertising. *Retail* and *classified advertising sales people* keep close track of clients and often provide pick-up service for advertising copy, handle changes in ads, and suggest advertising approaches.

On small newspapers, advertising may be sold by all members of the staff, or the paper may employ a part-time advertising sales person.

Magazines use national sales representatives even more than newspapers since most magazines have a wider, often national, distribution. Local and regional magazines employ more local sales people.

Radio stations employ *radio advertising sales people* to sell air time to local businesses and use national sales representatives on a commission basis to sell local time to national and regional advertisers. The radio advertising sales person sells radio time in the form of entire programs or portions of programs or spot announcements. He or she must know not only the type of audience that listens to a particular station but also the time of day that a very specific segment of the audience is most likely to be listening. Radio advertising sales people must be well versed in the latest market research analysis of their local marketing areas and must be prepared to advise a client on the best advertising approach for the money.

At small radio stations, everyone may sell advertising, or the station manager may handle all advertising. Larger stations employ several sales people, and those in large marketing areas may have large sales staffs.

The typical television station in a major city employs six to eight *television advertising sales people* to call on local businesses. A great deal of television advertising time is also sold by national sales representatives who have branch offices in major cities. These "sales reps" sell most television advertising and act as the go-between for local stations and the national advertisers.

Network sales people work for the national television and radio networks and sell network time to national advertisers. They handle accounts worth hundreds of thousands of dollars.

Places of Employment and Working Conditions   Advertising sales jobs can be found in all communities, with the most opportunities in large metropolitan areas. National sales representatives are concentrated in cities such as Chicago, Los Angeles, and New York.

Advertising sales is a combination of office, telephone, and leg work. The sales people work long hours. It is often necessary to spend a great deal of time on a particular account, including the preparation of sales presentations and cost estimates.

Qualifications, Education, and Training   The personal qualities of a good sales person include aggressiveness, enthusiasm, perseverance, and the ability to get along with people.

Sales experience of any kind is valuable, and experience in selling advertising is especially helpful.

Although a college degree is not required by all employers, large metropolitan newspapers, mass-circulation and trade magazines, major radio and television stations, networks, and national sales representative firms require a bachelor's degree in marketing or journalism. Some require a major in advertising.

Potential and Advancement
The future for magazine, newspaper, radio, and television advertising is very good. Media sales will continue to grow and provide many opportunities.

Beginners will find the best opportunities with small local newspapers and magazines and small radio and television stations where they can gain valuable experience. There will continue to be opportunities for part-time work with small newspapers and small or local radio and television stations.

Newspaper advertising sales people can advance to positions as general advertising manager, retail advertising manager, classified advertising manager, or advertising director.

Radio advertising sales people can advance to sales manager positions where they would be involved in developing sales plans as well as in developing policies and programming.

In television, advertising sales people can advance to regional, national, and general sales manager positions. The top-level positions in television station management are very often filled by former general sales managers.

Income
Advertising sales people work on a commission basis, and the amount of their earnings is governed by their own ability and ambition. Some employers provide a base salary plus a commission. Commission rates vary but are usually between 10 percent and 15 percent.

Sales managers on large magazines earn $31,000 to $50,000 a year. Newspaper space sales people earn from $21,000 to $48,000.

Radio advertising sales people average about $24,000 a year, with much higher earnings for network sales people.

Earnings of television national sales representatives are better than sales earnings in just about any other industry. Beginners can earn $25,000 to $37,000 in their first year, and earnings of experienced national sales people often approach six figures. They also take part in company stock or profit-sharing plans.

On a local level, television advertising sales people earn between $15,000 and $45,000 a year. Beginners can earn $14,000 to $20,000 a year; more experienced sales people earn between $25,000 and $32,000. Top local television sales people earn between $36,000 and $47,000. In the largest cities, these figures are even higher.

In all advertising sales fields the median income is about $28,000 a year.

Additional Sources of Information

Radio Advertising Bureau
304 Park Avenue, South
New York, NY 10010

National Association of Broadcasters
1771 N Street, NW
Washington, DC 20036

American Newspaper Publishers Association
P.O. Box 17407
Dulles International Airport
Washington, DC 20041

International Newspaper Advertising and Marketing Executives, Inc.
P.O. Box 17210
Washington, DC 20041

Television Bureau of Advertising
477 Madison Avenue
New York, NY 10022

Advertising Worker

The Job   For the thousands of people working in advertising, job satisfaction may come from having their work appear in print or on television or radio.

The work of a number of people with special talents goes into every advertising campaign, and the end result, when the campaign is successful, can make a great difference in the sales figures of a product or service.

Artists, designers, and layout artists create the visual aspects of advertising in magazine and newspaper ads, television commercials, and product packaging. They select photographs, draw illustrations, and decide on the colors and style of type to be used. They also prepare samples of art work for account executives who are planning advertising campaigns with clients and prospective clients.

Copywriters provide the words. A copywriter usually works closely with the account executive to produce just what the client wants to say about his or her product or service. The work of the copywriter is an integral part of almost all advertising but is especially important in radio where words are the *only* vehicle for the advertiser's message.

Production managers arrange for the actual filming, recording, or printing of the completed advertisement. They must be able to produce the finished product on time and within the budget allocated by the client. They normally deal with models, actors, and photographers.

Media buyers are specialists who are well informed on the costs and audiences of the various media. They work with account executives to decide on how to reach the largest and most appropriate consumer audience for a client's product or service. Working within the client's budget, they buy advertising time on radio or television and advertising space in newspapers and magazines. In some agencies, the functions are separated into *time buyers* and *space buyers*.

About 100,000 people are employed in advertising agencies, and two or three times that number work in the advertising departments of commercial and industrial firms, retail stores, and newspapers and magazines. Printing companies, package design firms, sign companies, and mail order catalogs also employ persons with advertising skills.

Beginners in advertising usually start as assistants in research, production, or media buying. Those with writing ability usually start as *junior copywriters*.

Related jobs are advertising account executive, advertising manager, advertising sales person, and marketing researcher.

Places of Employment and Working Conditions   About half of all advertising workers are employed in the New York City and Chicago areas, but opportunities exist in most cities.

All advertising workers function under a great deal of pressure. The usual 35- to 40-hour workweek often includes overtime because of deadlines, the demands of clients, and production schedules.

Although advertising agencies are considered the most glamorous places to work, there may be little job security in an agency. If an agency loses a big account, all the people who worked on the account, including the account executive, may lose their jobs.

Qualifications, Education, and Training   Creativity and a knowledge of what motivates consumers are the keys to success in advertising.

Successful advertising workers also have imagination, a flair for language, and the ability to sell ideas. They must get along well with people, be able to function as part of a team, enjoy challenge and variety, and thrive on excitement and competition.

High school courses in art and writing are valuable, as are experience in selling advertising for a school newspaper or a summer job at a radio station or newspaper office. Any education or professional experience in marketing, art, writing, journalism, or business and marketing research is valuable.

There are no specific educational requirements in the advertising field, but most employers prefer college graduates; they will accept a degree in almost any field. Some have a preference for a liberal arts background with majors in art, literature, and social sciences; others want applicants with degrees in marketing, business, or journalism. There are, however, more than 1000 colleges and universities in the United States that offer majors in advertising.

When seeking a position in advertising, certain job applicants are expected to provide samples of their work. A beginning artist should supply a portfolio of drawings; a writer should supply samples of written work. Experienced advertising workers should include samples of the work they have handled for previous employers.

Potential and Advancement

About 300,000 persons work in the advertising field, one-third of them in advertising agencies. This is a popular field with stiff competition for entry-level jobs and for jobs with the best companies. Job opportunities should increase steadily, but, since the amount of money spent on advertising is strongly affected by general business conditions, they may be more plentiful in some years than in others. Local television, radio, and newspapers are expected to increase their share of total advertising, while magazines, direct mail, and national newspapers are declining and will provide fewer job opportunities.

Opportunities for advancement usually exist within each specialty area. An artist or designer can become an art director; a copywriter can be promoted to copy chief. Advancement to management is possible from any of the specialties, and experienced advertising workers sometimes open their own advertising agencies.

Income

Entry-level jobs pay $15,000 to $22,000 a year, with top starting salaries going to outstanding liberal arts graduates. Junior layout artists earn about $15,000 to $19,000; junior copywriters about $18,000 to $23,000.

Average annual salaries for experienced advertising workers include senior layout artists, $30,000; art directors, $30,000; executive art directors, $39,000; production managers, $31,000; senior copywriters, $41,000. Media space or time buyers average from $19,000 to $24,000; media directors, $80,000. Highly experienced buyers earn more.

Top executive officers in advertising earn from $80,000 to $120,000 or more annually.

Additional Sources of Information

American Association of Advertising Agencies
666 Third Avenue
13th Floor
New York, NY 10017

American Advertising Federation
Education Services Department
1400 K Street, NW
Suite 1000
Washington, DC 20005

Airport Manager

The Job Whether it is a small local airport or an elaborate complex handling international flights, there has to be an airport manager in charge. An airport manager is responsible for the efficient day-to-day operation of the airport, including provisions for aircraft maintenance and fuel, condition and safety of runways and other facilities, budget and personnel, negotiation of leases with airport tenants such as airlines and terminal concessionaires, enforcement of airport and government regulations, recordkeeping, and public relations.

An airport manager must be familiar with state and federal regulations pertaining to airports and must strive to maintain good relations with local communities. An important part of the job is making local businesses and industries aware of the services available at the airport. In an airport operated by a local government agency, the airport manager may be responsible for reporting to a variety of boards or committees.

At a small installation, the owner-operator may handle all duties, while at a large airport the manager, or director, is assisted by a number of specialists, each of whom is responsible for specific areas of airport operation.

An *assistant airport director* assists the director or manager with administrative responsibilities and may be in charge of public relations, maintenance, personnel, or tenant relations. An *engineer* handles maintenance of runways, terminal buildings, hangars, and grounds. The engineer oversees new construction, handles real estate and zoning matters, and administers Federal Aid to Airports programs.

An important position at all but the smallest airports is that of *fixed based operator (FBO)*. At owner-operated airports, the manager may fulfill this function personally, but at other airports it is handled by a retail firm employing from one or two people to several hundred. The FBO provides (sells) general aviation products and/or services at an airport. This can include aircraft repair services, flight training, aircraft sales, fuel and spare parts, air taxi service, and charter flights.

Places of Employment and Working Conditions

Airport managers are employed throughout the United States in airports of all sizes. The most job opportunities are in California, Florida, Illinois, Indiana, Michigan, Missouri, New York, Ohio, Pennsylvania, and Texas.

In a small airport, the manager usually works long hours, many of them outdoors. At large facilities, the manager usually works regular hours in an office but is on call for emergency situations. Managers do some traveling in the course of their work as they negotiate with airport tenants, such as airlines, or when they appear before state and federal regulatory agencies. Community activities and meetings usually require some evening hours.

Qualifications, Education, and Training

Leadership qualities, tact, initiative, good judgment, and the ability to get along with people are important qualities. Managers of airports with airline service usually need a college degree in airport management, business or public administration, or aeronautical or civil engineering. Colleges and universities that offer these degrees sometimes offer flight training as well.

At smaller airports, experience as a fixed base operator or superintendent of maintenance plus a pilot's license are often sufficient for the position of airport manager.

Potential and Advancement

There are approximately 13,000 airports of various sizes in the United States. Substantial growth is expected in this field as existing airports are enlarged and new ones built to handle increased passenger travel, air cargo tonnage, and general aviation activity.

The present heavy air traffic at major airports, which creates takeoff and landing delays, is expected to lead to the construction of a network of smaller satellite airports to service general aviation aircraft and helicopters that will ferry passengers to and from the major airports. Both airport managers and fixed based operators will be in demand for these new facilities.

Advancement in this field usually takes the form of moving to a larger airport with more complex responsibilities. Some airport managers move up to state or federal positions in regulatory agencies.

Income   Earnings range from about $18,000 at a small general aviation airport to over $63,000 at a major international airport.

Additional Sources of Information

Airport Operators Council International
1700 K Street, NW
Washington, DC 20036

Office of General Aviation
Federal Aviation Administration
Washington, DC 20591

Architect

The Job   An architect designs buildings and other structures—anything from a private home to a large office building or an entire city's redevelopment.

The architect must oversee all phases of the project, from initial idea to completed structure. He or she must solve complex technical problems while retaining artistic design and must be able to function in a highly competitive atmosphere.

After discussing ideas, needs, and concepts with the client, the architect prepares preliminary drawings and then detailed plans for the project, including the plumbing, electrical, and heating systems. He or she must specify materials that comply with local building regulations and must stay within the client's budget.

All through this process, the architect may have to make changes at the request of the client. Once plans are ready and approved, the architect may help the client select a contractor and will continue to check the work while it is in progress to ensure that all design specifications are being carried out. The architect's responsibility does not end until the structure is completed and has successfully passed all required inspections.

Architects can work in salaried positions for architectural firms, or they can go into private practice. Those who decide to open their own businesses usually begin their careers with a few years in salaried positions in order to accumulate experience.

Most architects are employed by architectural firms, building contractors, and community planning and redevelopment authorities. A few architects work for government agencies such as the Department of Defense, Housing and Urban Development, and the General Services Administration.

Because this is a field where part-time practice is possible and since architects often work from their homes, the field has advantages for people with family responsibilities.

Related fields are building contractor and urban planner.

Places of Employment and Working Conditions
Architects are employed throughout the country, in towns and cities of all sizes. A large proportion of all architectural work, however, is concentrated in Boston, Chicago, Los Angeles, New York City, Philadelphia, San Francisco, and Washington, DC.

Architects spend many hours drawing plans and sometimes must put in overtime to meet deadlines. Once building is under way, they spend a great deal of time outdoors inspecting the progress of construction.

Qualifications, Education, and Training
Architecture requires a wide variety of technical, artistic, and social skills. Anyone planning a career in this field should be able to work independently, have a capacity for solving technical problems, and be artistic. Good business skills are also very helpful.

High school students interested in architecture should take courses in mathematics, physics, and art. Summer jobs with architects or building contractors can provide useful experience.

Over half of all architects are graduates of a five-year program leading to a bachelor of architecture degree; however, there are several types of professional programs in architecture, with some leading to master's degrees. Ninety-six schools of architecture are accredited by the National Architectural Accrediting Board. Courses typically include architectural theory, design, graphics, engineering, urban planning, English, mathematics, chemistry, sociology, economics, and a foreign language.

Although many architects work without a license, all states require that a licensed architect take the final legal responsibility for a completed project. To become licensed, the architect must have a professional degree in architecture, a period of practical training or internship (usually three years), and passing scores on all sections of the Architect Registration Examination.

Potential and Advancement
There are approximately 108,000 architects in the United States at present. Prospects for employment in architecture are currently good, but depend upon the number of degrees being granted and the rise and fall of the building market. With an increase in schools that

grant architectural degrees and a growing interest in more efficient housing and public construction, jobs will be available, but competition is expected to be keen.

New graduates usually begin as junior drafters and work their way up to increased responsibility. They may be promoted to chief or senior drafter or put in charge of one phase of a large project such as design, specification writing, or construction supervision.

Income   Median annual earnings for experienced architects are about $36,100. Those who are associates in their firms may also receive a share of the profits in addition to their salary. Principals or partners of firms earn a median salary of $57,700, with partners in some large practices earning over $100,000.

The median salary for intern architects is $24,000 annually.

Additional Sources of Information

The American Institute of Architects
1735 New York Avenue, NW
Washington, DC 20006

The Association of Collegiate Schools of Architecture, Inc.
1735 New York Avenue, NW
Washington, DC 20006

The National Council of Architectural Registration Boards
1735 New York Avenue, NW
Suite 700
Washington, DC 20006

Bank Officer

The Job   Bank officers are responsible for carrying out the policies set by the board of directors of the bank and for overseeing the day-to-day operations of all the banking departments. A thorough knowledge of business and economics is necessary, plus expertise in the specialized banking area for which each officer is responsible.

Bank officers and their responsibilities include: *loan officer,* who evaluates the credit and collateral of individuals and businesses applying for loans; *trust officer,* who administers estates and trusts, manages property, invests funds for customers, and provides financial counseling; *operations officer,* who plans and coordinates procedures and systems; *branch manager,* who is responsible for all functions of a branch office; *international officer,* who handles financial dealings abroad or for foreign customers; and *cashier,* who is responsible for all bank property. Other officers handle auditing, personnel administration, public relations, and operations research. In small banks there may be only a few officers, each of whom handles several functions or departments.

Places of Employment and Working Conditions   Bank officers are employed in towns and cities of all sizes throughout the country.

Bank officers are usually involved in the civic and business affairs of their communities and are often called upon to serve as directors of local companies and community organizations. This can entail evenings spent away from home attending meetings and functions related to these positions.

Qualifications, Education, and Training   The ability to inspire confidence in others is a necessary characteristic of a successful bank officer. Officers should also display tact and good judgment in dealing with customers and employees. The ability to work independently and to analyze information are also important.

High school students interested in banking should study mathematics and take any available courses in economics.

Potential bank officers usually start their careers at a bank by entering the bank's management training program after graduation from college. Occasionally, outstanding clerks and tellers work their way up the ladder through promotions and are also accepted into these training programs, but the usual background is a college degree.

The ideal preparation for a banking officer has been described as a bachelor's degree in social science along with a master of business administration degree. A business administration degree with a major in finance, or a liberal arts degree with courses in accounting, economics, commercial law, political science, and statistics, are also good college backgrounds.

Potential and Advancement   Employment is expected to increase substantially. Banking is one of the fastest-growing industries in our economy;

expanding bank services and the increased use of computers will continue to require trained personnel in all areas of banking.

It usually takes many years of experience to advance to senior officer and management positions. Experience in several banking departments, as well as continuing education in management-sponsored courses, can aid and accelerate promotion.

Income   Income varies, with banks in large cities paying more than those in small towns.

Management trainees usually earn about $19,000 a year. Those with an MBA degree can command starting salaries of $27,000 a year. Senior bank officers earn annual salaries of $60,000 or more.

Additional Sources of Information

American Bankers Association
Bank Personnel Division
1120 Connecticut Avenue, NW
Washington, DC 20036

National Association of Bank Women
National Office
500 North Michigan Avenue
Suite 1400
Chicago, IL 60611

National Bankers Association
122 C Street, NW
Suite 580
Washington, DC 20001

Federal Deposit Insurance Corporation
Director of Personnel
550 17th Street, NW
Washington, DC 20429

Board of Governors
The Federal Reserve System
Personnel Department
Washington, DC 20551

Bank Worker

The Job   Banks employ the same clerical workers as other businesses and industries—file clerks, stenographers, secretaries, typists, and receptionists. But there are two groups of clerical employees that perform duties unique to the banking industry—clerks and tellers.

Bank clerks are responsible for all the records of the monetary activities of the bank and its customers. They have specialized duties and often use office machines that are designed especially for banking functions. Their titles include sorter, proof machine operator, bookkeeping machine operator, bookkeeping and accounting clerk, transit clerk, interest clerk, and mortgage clerk. With the wide use of electronic data processing equipment in the banking industry, bank clerk occupations also now include such jobs as electronic reader-sorter operator, check inscriber or encoder, control clerk, coding clerk, tape librarian, and teletype operator.

Tellers are the most visible employees of a bank and should project an efficient, pleasant, and dependable image, both for themselves and for their employer. Tellers cash checks, handle deposits and withdrawals, sell savings bonds and traveler's checks, keep records, and handle paperwork. In the course of this work, they must be thorough and accurate in checking identification, verifying accounts and money amounts, and counting out money to customers. At the end of their working day, all transactions must balance.

Some opportunities for part-time teller work exist in larger banks. These extra tellers are used during peak banking hours and on peak banking days.

Places of Employment and Working Conditions   Bank clerks and tellers work in all areas of the country, in communities of all sizes.

In small banks, clerks and tellers usually perform a variety of duties, while in large banks they work in one specialty area. Boredom can be a problem in some of the clerical functions, and some bank workers object to the close supervision that is part of their working atmosphere.

Tellers stand on their feet during much of their workday; anyone who does not like to be confined to a small space might find the teller cages of some banks unpleasant.

Qualifications, Education, and Training   Personal qualities of honesty and integrity are necessary for a job in banking. A fondness for working with numbers, attention to detail, and the ability to work as part of a closely supervised team are essential. Tellers should have a pleasant personality and like to work with people.

A high school diploma is adequate preparation for entry-level jobs, especially if the applicant has had courses in typing, bookkeeping, office machine operation, and business arithmetic.

Banks usually train beginning clerks to operate various office machines. Tellers receive anywhere from a few days to three weeks or more of training and spend some time observing an experienced teller before handling any work on their own.

Bank training courses are available to all bank employees throughout their working years. Employees who avail themselves of these courses can advance by gaining new skills. The successful completion of specific banking courses can lead to promotion.

Potential and Advancement

There are about 517,000 persons working as bank tellers. Numerous closings, mergers, and consolidations in the banking industry will lead to a decline in the number of bank tellers through the year 2005. The increasing efficiency brought about by automatic teller machines and on-line video terminals will also contribute to this decline. However, there are still good opportunities for qualified persons because this is a large profession with a high rate of job turnover.

Bank clerks may be promoted to supervisory positions within their own specialty area, to teller or credit analyst, and eventually to senior supervisory positions. Tellers can advance to head teller. Additional education, in the form of courses offered by the American Institute of Banking, can aid advancement, and outstanding clerks and tellers who have college training in addition to banking courses can sometimes advance to bank officers.

Income

Median annual earnings of full-time tellers are $14,200. The lowest 10 percent earn about $10,000, while the top 10 percent earn around $21,500. In general, a greater range of responsibilities results in a higher salary. However, experience, length of service, and, especially, the location and size of the bank are also important.

Additional Sources of Information

American Bankers Association
1120 Connecticut Avenue, NW
Washington, DC 20036

Institute of Financial Education
111 East Wacker Drive
Chicago, IL 60601

Building or Property Manager

The Job   A building or property manager is responsible for overseeing the day-to-day happenings of a building with multiple tenants, such as office buildings, apartment houses, or shopping centers.

A building or property manager is a combination of administrator, rental agent, accountant, public relations expert, purchasing agent, and maintenance person. The manager may simply have an office on the premises, or he or she may live there in an apartment supplied by the owners of the building.

In a single building with only a handful of tenants, the manager handles everything with the help of a small clerical and maintenance staff. In large units, the manager supervises a large staff that handles the details of maintenance, security, leases and rent collection, accounting, and other matters.

One of the most important duties of a building manager is securing tenants for the facility. That involves showing available units to prospective tenants, arranging leases, and providing renovations to suit commercial tenants. Each of these activities is of prime importance to the profitable operation of the building. The reputation of the building manager and staff for competence and service may influence the prospective tenant's decision to move into a building.

Most building managers are employed by real estate and development firms, banks or trust companies, or insurance companies that own investment property. Government agencies employ building managers in subsidized public housing projects. Some building managers are self-employed.

A beginner in this field usually works under the supervision of an experienced manager. To gain experience, the beginner might be given responsibility for a small building or hired as a resident supervisor or maintenance manager.

A related job is real estate agent/broker.

Places of Employment and Working Conditions   Building managers must recognize that tenants can sometimes be demanding, troublesome, and unreasonable, and the building manager is on call at all times for emergencies and problems.

Qualifications, Education, and Training   Reliability, good judgment, tact, and diplomacy are all necessary. A building manager must also have initiative and a well-developed sales ability.

High school preparation should include business courses and the development of communication skills.

A college education is becoming more and more important in this field. A background in accounting, law, finance, management, government, or economics is helpful; a business degree with a major in real estate is ideal. Junior and community colleges offer two-year programs leading to an associate degree, which is also acceptable to many employers.

As in all real estate jobs, continuing education is important. A number of organizations offer courses in all parts of the country at frequent intervals. Those who have adequate education and experience can receive a formal professional designation upon completion of certain courses and examinations.

Potential and Advancement   Experienced building managers are always in demand. Large metropolitan areas, retirement and resort communities, and industrial areas all provide numerous job opportunities. Opportunities will be best for those with college degrees in business administration or a related field.

Advancement usually takes the form of increased responsibility in larger buildings or management firms. Some experienced managers go into business for themselves, and many of them eventually go into real estate investing.

Income   Earnings vary greatly depending on geographic area, size of buildings, and level of responsibility. Median annual earnings for all property managers are $21,800, with the middle 50 percent earning between $14,600 and $33,600.

On-site apartment managers average $31,300 yearly, while those managing multiple apartment complexes average $63,000. Shopping center property managers average $69,300 annually, and office building managers average $72,200.

Additional Sources of Information

Building Owners and Managers Institute International
1521 Ritchie Highway
Arnold, MD 21012

Institute of Real Estate Management
430 North Michigan Avenue
Chicago, IL 60611

Apartment Owners and Managers Association of America
65 Cherry Plaza
Watertown, CT 06795

City Manager

The Job A city manager, usually appointed by the elected officials of a community, administers and coordinates the day-to-day activities of the community. The city manager oversees such functions as tax collection and disbursement, law enforcement, public works, budget preparation, studies of current problems, and planning for future needs. In a small city, the manager handles all functions; in a larger city, the manager usually has a number of assistants, each of whom manages a department.

City managers and their assistants supervise city employees, coordinate city programs, greet visitors, answer correspondence, prepare reports, represent the city at public hearings and meetings, analyze work procedures, and prepare budgets.

Most city managers work for small cities (under 25,000) that have a council-manager type of government. The council, which is elected, hires the manager, who is then responsible for running the city as well as for hiring a staff. In cities with a mayor-council type of government, the mayor hires the city manager as his or her top administrative assistant.

A few managers work for counties and for metropolitan and regional planning bodies.

Most city managers begin as management assistants in one of the city departments such as finance, public works, or planning. Experience in several different departments is valuable and can provide a well-rounded background.

This is a new and growing profession with room for people trained in a variety of disciplines that relate to the functions and problems of urban life.

Places of Employment and Working Conditions City managers are employed throughout the country in cities of all sizes, but job opportunities are greatest in the eastern states.

Working conditions for a city manager are usually those of an office position with considerable public contact. More than 40 hours a week are usually required, and emergency situations and public meetings frequently involve evening and weekend work.

Qualifications, Education, and Training Persons planning a career in city management must be dedicated to public service and willing to work as part of a team. They should have self-confidence, be able to analyze

problems and suggest solutions, and function well under stress. Tact and the ability to communicate well are very important.

A graduate degree is presently required even for most entry-level positions in this field. An undergraduate degree in a field such as engineering, recreation, social work, or political science should be followed by a master's degree in public or municipal administration or business administration.

Requirements in some of the 185 colleges and universities that offer advanced degrees in this field include an internship of six months to a year, in which the candidate must work in a city manager's office to gain experience.

Potential and Advancement   Approximately 11,000 persons are presently employed as city managers and assistants, and the field is growing rapidly. However, job competition is expected to be very strong over the next few years, due to an increase in the number of graduates in this field.

Recent computerized management techniques for taxes, traffic control, and utility billing will create openings for those trained in finance, while increasing emphasis on broad solutions to urban social problems will result in opportunities for those with a strong public administration background. Also, the council-manager system of government is the fastest growing type in the country, and the move is toward professional, rather than elected, city management.

Generally, one begins as an assistant to a city manager or department head with promotions leading to greater responsibility. A city manager will probably work in several different types and sizes of cities in his or her career, which will further broaden the person's experience and promotion potential.

Income   Salaries for city managers depend on education, experience, job responsibility, and the size of the employing city. Salaries are generally high; the average annual salary is over $57,000. Salaries range from $33,000 a year in towns with populations of fewer than 2,500 to $125,000 in cities of more than 1 million.

Benefits usually include travel expenses and a car for official business.

Additional Sources of Information

International City Management Association
777 North Capitol Street, NE
Suite 500
Washington, DC 20002

Claim Representative

The Job   Claim representatives, including both claim adjusters and claim examiners, investigate claims for insurance companies, negotiate settlements with policyholders, and authorize payment of claims.

Claim adjusters work for property-liability (casualty) insurance companies and usually specialize in specific types of claims such as fire, marine, or automobile. They determine whether their company is liable (that is, whether the customer's claim is a valid one covered by the customer's policy) and recommend the amount of settlement. In the course of investigating a claim, adjusters consider physical evidence, testimony of witnesses, and any applicable reports. They strive to protect their company from false or inflated claims and at the same time settle valid claims quickly and fairly. In some companies, adjusters submit their findings to *claim examiners*, who then review them and authorize payment.

In states with "no-fault" auto insurance, adjusters do not have to establish responsibility for a loss but must decide the amount of the loss. Many auto insurance companies employ special inside adjusters who settle smaller claims by mail or telephone or at special drive-in centers where claims can be settled immediately.

Most claim adjusters work for insurance companies, but some work for independent firms that contract their services to insurance companies for a fee. These firms vary in size from local firms employing two or three adjusters to large national organizations with hundreds of adjustment specialists.

A few adjusters represent the insured rather than the insurance company. These "public" adjusters are retained by banks, financial organizations, and other businesses to negotiate settlements with insurance companies.

In life insurance companies, claim examiners are the equivalent of claim adjusters. In the course of settling a claim, an examiner might correspond with policyholders or their families, consult medical specialists, calculate benefit payments, and review claim applications for completeness. Questionable claims or those exceeding a specified amount would be even more thoroughly investigated by the examiner.

Claim examiners also maintain records of settled claims and prepare reports for company data processing departments. More experienced examiners serve on company committees, survey claim settlement procedures, and work to improve the efficiency of claim handling departments.

Related jobs are actuary, insurance agent and broker, and underwriter.

Places of Employment and Working Conditions   Claim adjusters work in all sections of the United States, in cities and towns of all sizes.

Claim examiners, on the other hand, work in the home offices of insurance companies, most of which are located in and around Boston, Chicago, Dallas, New York City, Philadelphia, and San Francisco.

Adjusters make their own schedules, doing whatever is necessary to dispose of a claim promptly and fairly. Since most firms provide 24-hour claim service, adjusters are on call all the time and may work some weekends and evenings. They may be called to the site of an accident, fire, or burglary or to the scene of a riot or hurricane. They must be physically fit since they spend much of their day traveling, climbing stairs, and actively investigating claims. Much of their time is spent out-of-doors—this is not a desk job.

Claim examiners, by contrast, do have desk jobs. Their usual workweek is 35 to 40 hours, but they may work longer hours during peak claim loads or when quarterly and annual reports are prepared. They may travel occasionally in the course of their investigations and are sometimes called upon to testify in court regarding contested claims.

Qualifications, Education, and Training

Claim representatives should be able to communicate tactfully and effectively. They need a good memory and should enjoy working with details. Claim examiners must also be familiar with medical and legal terms, insurance laws and regulations, and have mathematical skills.

Insurance companies prefer to hire college graduates for positions as claim representatives but will sometimes hire those with specialized experience, such as individuals with automobile repair experience for automobile claims adjuster positions. Because of the complexity of insurance regulations and claim procedures, however, claim representatives without a college degree may advance more slowly than those with two years or more of college.

Many large insurance companies provide on-the-job training combined with home-study courses for newly hired claim adjusters and claim examiners. Throughout their careers, claim representatives continue to take a variety of courses and programs designed to certify them in many different areas of the profession.

Licensing of adjusters is required in most states. Requirements vary, but applicants usually must be 20 or 21 years of age and a resident of the state, complete an approved training course in insurance or loss adjusting, provide character references, pass a written examination, and file a surety bond (a bond guaranteeing performance of a contract or obligation).

Potential and Advancement

About 141,500 persons are employed as claim representatives. While all indications point to continued growth of the insurance industry and a continued need for claim representatives, persons trying to enter the field will have an advantage if they have certain specialized skills.

The growing trend toward drive-in claim centers and claim handling by telephone will probably reduce the demand for automobile adjusters but increase the demand for inside adjusters. Those who specialize in workers' compensation, product liability, and other types of complex business insurance will be more in demand than ever. Job opportunities for claim examiners are becoming more numerous in property-liability companies than in life insurance companies, where computers are processing more and more of the routine claims and group policy claims.

Claim representatives are promoted as they gain experience and complete courses and training programs. Those who demonstrate unusual ability or administrative skills may become department supervisors or may advance to management jobs. Some qualified adjusters, however, prefer to broaden their knowledge by transferring to other departments such as underwriting or sales.

Income   Inside adjusters working for property-liability companies earn a median salary of $24,500 a year, and senior inside adjusters earn $30,000. Sometimes adjusters are also given a company car or are reimbursed for using their own vehicle for business purposes.

Claim examiners earn a median annual salary of $30,800; senior claim examiners earn $35,500; claim supervisors, $43,300; and claim managers, $53,900.

Claim representatives working for large insurance companies usually have life and health insurance and retirement plans. Paid holidays are more numerous in the insurance industry than in most other industries, and two-week paid vacations are usual after one year of service. In most large companies, employees receive three weeks of paid vacation after five years.

Additional Sources of Information

Insurance Information Institute
110 William Street
New York, NY 10038

American Mutual Insurance Alliance
20 North Wacker Drive
Chicago, IL 60606

National Association of Independent Insurance Adjusters
22 West Adams Street
Room 845
Chicago, IL 60606

National Association of Public Adjusters
300 Water Street
Baltimore, MD 21202

Life Office Management Association
5770 Powers Ferry Road
Atlanta, GA 30327

Computer Programmer

The Job   Computer programmers write detailed instructions, called programs, that list the orderly steps a computer must follow to solve a problem. Once programming is completed, the programmer runs a sample of the data to make sure the program is correct and will produce the desired information. This is called "debugging." If there are any errors, the program must be changed and rechecked until it produces the correct results. The final step is the preparation of an instruction sheet for the computer operator who will be running the program.

A simple program can be written and debugged in a few days. Those that use many data files or complex mathematical formulas may require a year or more of work. On such large projects, several programmers work together under the supervision of an experienced programmer.

Programmers usually work from problem descriptions prepared by *systems analysts* who have examined the problem and determined the next steps necessary to solve it. In organizations that do not employ systems analysts, employees called *programmer-analysts* handle both functions. An *applications programmer* then writes detailed instructions for programming the data. Applications programmers usually specialize in business or scientific work.

A *systems programmer* is a specialist who maintains the general instructions (software) that control the operation of the entire computer system.

Beginners in this field spend several months working under supervision before they begin to handle all aspects of the job.

Most programmers are employed by manufacturing firms, banks, insurance companies, data processing services, utilities, and government agencies. Systems programmers usually work in research organizations, computer manufacturing firms, and large computer centers.

Places of Employment and Working Conditions
Programmers are employed in all areas of the country.

Most programmers work a 40-hour week, but their hours are not always 9:00 to 5:00. They may occasionally work on weekends or at other odd hours to have access to the computer when it is not needed for scheduled work.

Qualifications, Education, and Training
Patience, persistence, and accuracy are necessary characteristics for a programmer. Ingenuity, imagination, and the ability to think logically are also important.

High school experience should include as many mathematics and computer courses as possible.

There are no standard training requirements for programmers. Depending on the work to be done, an employer may require only some special courses in computer programming or a college education or a graduate degree in computer science, mathematics, or engineering.

Computer programming courses are offered by vocational and technical schools, colleges and universities, and junior colleges. Home-study courses are also available, and a few high schools offer some training in programming.

Scientific organizations require college training; some require advanced degrees in computer science, mathematics, engineering, or the physical sciences.

Because of rapidly changing technologies, programmers take periodic training courses offered by employers, software vendors, and computer manufacturers. Like physicians, they must keep constantly abreast of the latest developments in their field. These courses also aid in advancement and promotion.

Potential and Advancement
There are about 565,000 computer programmers. This is a rapidly growing field because of the expanding use of computers. Simpler programming needs will be increasingly handled by improved software so that programmers with only the most basic training will not find as many job openings as in the recent past. A strong demand will continue, however, for college graduates with a major in computer science or a related field. Graduates of two-year programs should find ample job openings in the business world.

There are many opportunities for advancement in this field. In large organizations, programmers may be promoted to lead programmers with supervisory responsibilities. Both applications programmers and systems programmers can be promoted to systems analyst positions.

Income
Programmers earn median annual salaries of about $34,000, with the middle 50 percent earning between $25,700 and $42,300. Some programmers earn over $50,000 annually.

Programmers who work in the West and Northeast earn more than those in the South and Midwest.

Additional Sources of Information

Data Processing Management Association
505 Busse Highway
Park Ridge, IL 60068

American Federation of Information Processing Societies
1899 Preston White Drive
Reston, VA 22091

Association for Computing Machinery
11 West 42d Street
New York, NY 10036

Controller

The Job The briefest and broadest definition of a controller (or the comptroller) is the key financial executive who controls, analyzes, and interprets the financial results and records of a company or an organization.

The *treasurer,* on the other hand, is responsible for the receipt, custody, and properly organized disbursement of an organization's or company's funds.

Some organizations also have a *vice president of finance* who has overall financial responsibility and reports to the chief executive officer—president or chairman of the board—of the company.

A company may have one or all of these financial officers or may combine all three into one executive-level position with any of the above titles. This job description will be confined to the usual duties of a controller in an organization that has a separate treasurer position.

The controller is responsible for the design of a company's accounting system(s), the preparation of budgets and financial forecasts, internal auditing of company operations and records, controls of company funds kept by the treasurer, establishment and administration of tax policies and procedures, and preparation of reports made to government agencies. Since an organization's financial operations involve the accumulation, interpretation, and storage of vast amounts of detailed information, a controller is very often in charge of the company's computerized data processing operation, too.

Places of Employment and Working Conditions Controllers are employed throughout the country. They work for government agencies, businesses, industry, nonprofit organizations, hospitals, and other institutions of all sizes.

As with many top-level jobs, controllers often work long hours under great pressure. Peak work loads occur when tax reports and stockholders' reports are prepared.

Qualifications, Education, and Training A controller needs more than facility with mathematics and the ability to do accurate work. At this level of responsibility, good judgment, planning ability, administrative and management skills, ability to motivate other people, and communication skills must be combined with expertise in cost accounting, budgeting, taxes, and other specialized areas.

A college background in finance, accounting, economics, mathematics, or business administration is usually the basic education for this field. The majority of people who reach this level have a master's degree in business administration or a CPA (certified public accountant) certificate (see accountant job description for information on CPA requirements).

Potential and Advancement The career paths to the post of controller are varied. Cost analysis and accounting, budgeting, tax auditing, financial analysis, planning and programming, credit collections, systems and procedures, and data processing are all training grounds for executive-level financial positions.

Once the top management level has been reached, the usual method of advancement for a controller is to transfer to a larger organization where the responsibilities are greater and more complex. Some advance by moving from a top financial position in a large organization to the chief executive post in a smaller one. About 30 percent of all chief executive officers come up through the financial area.

Income Financial compensation at this level is excellent. The median annual salary is $35,800. In large companies, the controller very often has a six-figure income.

Additional Sources of Information

Financial Executives Institute
P.O. Box 1938
Morristown, NJ 07962

Economist

The Job Economists study and analyze the relationship between the supply and demand of goods and services and how they are produced, distributed, and consumed.

Over half of all economists work in private industry or businesses such as manufacturing firms, banks, insurance companies, securities and investment firms, and management consulting firms. They provide information to management that affects decisions on the marketing and pricing of company products, such as long- and short-term economic forecasts, and the effect of government policies on business.

Some economists are employed by colleges and universities where they teach or are engaged in research and writing. These economists are often called upon to act as consultants to business firms and to government agencies.

Many economists are employed in government; they prepare studies to assess economic conditions and the need for changes in government policies. They usually work in the fields of agriculture, forestry, business, finance, labor, transportation, and international trade and development.

Places of Employment and Working Conditions
Economists work primarily in large cities and in university towns. The largest concentrations are in the New York City, Chicago, and Washington, DC, metropolitan areas.

Qualifications, Education, and Training
Anyone interested in this career field should be able to work accurately and in detail since economics entails careful analysis of data. Good communications skills are also necessary.

High school should include as many mathematics courses as possible.

A college major in economics, mathematics, or a related social science is the basic preparation for a career in economics. Students should also study statistics and computer science. A bachelor's degree is sufficient for many beginning research, administrative, management trainee, and sales jobs. However, graduate school is increasingly necessary for advancement.

Graduate training in a specialty area such as advanced economic theory, labor economics, or international economics is necessary for college teaching positions. The larger colleges and universities require a Ph.D.

Potential and Advancement   There are about 37,000 economists in the United States. Some growth is expected in this field, but not all areas of economics will experience the same rate of growth. Colleges and universities will provide job openings on a limited basis, usually to replace economists who leave the occupation. Federal job opportunities should increase slowly; state and local governments will offer more opportunities. Private industry and business will continue to provide the largest number of job openings.

Advancement in this field usually requires advanced degrees.

Income   New graduates with a bachelor's degree earn an average starting salary of $25,200 a year. Those with a Ph.D. earn a median annual salary of $67,500; those with a master's degree, $54,000. Experienced workers with a bachelor's degree earn a median annual salary of $41,700.

Additional Sources of Information

Joint Council on Economic Education
432 Park Avenue South
New York, NY 10016

National Association of Business Economists
28790 Chagrin Boulevard
Suite 300
Cleveland, OH 44122

Hospital Administrator

The Job   The exact title may vary from institution to institution—with some calling their chief executive a director, superintendent, executive vice president, or president—but the responsibilities are the same. The administrator must provide the managerial skills necessary to run a hospital or health care facility with all its complex and varied departments and functions. To accomplish this, the administrator must have a working knowledge of all departments and their relationship to each other.

The administrator must staff the hospital with both medical and nonmedical personnel; provide all aspects of patient care services; purchase supplies and equipment; plan space allocations; and arrange for housekeeping items such as laundry, security, and maintenance. The administrator must also provide and work within a budget; act as liaison between the directors of the hospital and the medical staff; keep up with developments in the health care field, including government regulations; handle hospital community relations; and sometimes act as a fund raiser.

In large facilities, the administrator has a staff of assistants with expertise in a variety of fields, but, in small and medium-sized institutions, the administrator is responsible for all of them.

In addition to working in hospitals, health care administrators are employed by nursing homes and extended-care facilities, community health centers, mental health centers, outreach clinics, city or county health departments, and health maintenance organizations (HMOs). Others are employed as advisors and specialists by insurance companies, government regulatory agencies, and professional standards organizations such as the American Cancer Society and the American Heart Association. Some serve as commissioned officers in the medical service and hospitals of the various armed forces or work for the U.S. Public Health Service or Department of Veterans Affairs.

Depending on the size of the institution, a new graduate might start as an administrative assistant, an assistant administrator, a specialist in a specific management area, a department head, or an assistant department head. In a small health care facility, the new graduate would start in a position with broad responsibilities, while in a large hospital the position might be narrow in scope with rotating work in several departments necessary to gain broad experience.

Places of Employment and Working Conditions

Hospital administrators work throughout the country in hospitals and health care facilities of all sizes.

Administrators put in a full day, usually 60 hours or more a week. They are on call at all times for emergency situations that affect the functioning of the institution. They carry very heavy work loads and are constantly under a great deal of pressure.

Qualifications, Education, and Training

Administrators should have health and vitality, maturity, sound judgment, tact, patience, the ability to motivate others, good communication skills, and sensitivity for people.

Good grades in high school are important. Courses should include English, science, mathematics, business, public speaking, and social studies. Volunteer work or a part-time job in a hospital is helpful.

Preparation for this career includes four years of college plus two years of special graduate training. Above-average college grades are necessary to gain entry into a graduate program. In general, courses in economics, accounting, statistics, finance, psychology, political science, and as many liberal arts courses as possible are recommended. While some graduate programs require a liberal arts or social science background, others require a college background in business or health administration. There are currently 29 colleges and universities offering bachelor's degrees in health services administration and 60 accredited master's-degree programs.

The administrators of nursing homes must be licensed. In all states, nursing home administrators must pass an examination, complete a state-approved training program, and pursue continuing education.

Potential and Advancement

There are about 257,000 persons working in some phase of hospital administration, but only a relatively small number of these work at the upper levels of hospital and health care administration. The field is expected to expand rapidly, with the best opportunities in large hospitals with subsidiaries that provide services such as alcohol and drug abuse treatment, hospices, and home health care. There will be keen competition for upper-level administration jobs.

Hospital administrators are already in the top level of their profession, and advancement usually takes the form of moving to a larger institution with an increase in responsibility. Advancement is also achieved by moving from a single area of responsibility in a large institution to the top post in a small hospital.

Income   Earnings in this field cover a wide range, depending on the size of the hospital or health care facility, geographic location, health services provided, and responsibilities of the administrator.

The median annual salary for administrators of group practices is $58,000. Median salaries for administrators range from $40,200 in small practices to $96,000 in very large group practices. Half of those in the top positions in hospitals earn $121,500 or more; those at the bottom of the range earn less than $71,000, while those at the top of the range earn $203,400 or more.

Fringe benefits for administrators in hospitals of all sizes are often comparable to those of top executives in industry.

Additional Sources of Information

American College of Healthcare Executives
840 North Lake Shore Drive
Chicago, IL 60611

American Hospital Association
840 North Lake Shore Drive
Chicago, IL 60611

Association of University Programs in Health Administration
1911 North Fort Myer Drive
Suite 503
Arlington, VA 22209

Hotel/Motel Manager

The Job   The manager of a hotel or motel is responsible for the profitable operation of the facility and for the comfort and satisfaction of the guests.

The manager is responsible for setting room rates and credit policies, the operation of the kitchen and dining rooms, and the housekeeping, accounting, and maintenance departments. In a large hotel or motel, the manager may have several assistants who manage some parts of the operation, while in small facilities the manager may handle all aspects of the business personally, including front-desk clerical work such as taking reservations. This is especially true in owner operated facilities.

Many hotel and motel managers are self-employed. A significant number work for large hotel and motel chains.

Places of Employment and Working Conditions
Managers and their families very often live in the hotel or motel they manage and are on call at all times. Owner-operators often work very long hours.

Qualifications, Education, and Training
Initiative, self-discipline, and a knack for organization are indispensable in this field. Summer or part-time work in a hotel or motel is helpful.

Although small hotels and motels do not have specific educational requirements, they do require experience for manager positions. Some employers, especially in larger facilities, require a bachelor's degree or some type of postsecondary training in hotel management.

Training is also available at many junior and community colleges and technical institutes.

Some large hotels have on-the-job management programs in which trainees rotate among various departments to acquire a thorough knowledge of the hotel's operation.

Potential and Advancement
There are about 102,000 hotel and motel managers, and the field is expected to grow rapidly through the year 2005. More hotels and motels will be built as business travel continues to grow and domestic and foreign tourism increase. Most openings will occur to replace those who retire or leave the field. Those applicants with a college degree in hotel administration will have the best job opportunities.

Income
Salaries of hotel and motel managers depend on the size, location, and sales volume of the facility.

Assistant hotel managers earn, on average, $31,000 annually. Those working in large hotels earn over $36,000 and those working in small hotels average less than $25,000.

Experienced managers average nearly $56,000 a year, ranging from $42,300 in small hotels to about $81,800 in large hotels. Managers may also earn bonuses and may be provided with lodging, meals, laundry, and other services for themselves and their families.

Additional Sources of Information

The American Hotel and Motel Association (AH & MA)
Information Center
1201 New York Avenue, NW
Washington, DC 20005

Council on Hotel, Restaurant, and Institutional Education
1200 17th Street, NW
Washington, DC 20036

The Educational Institute of AH & MA
P.O. Box 1240
East Lansing, MI 48826

National Executive Housekeepers Association, Inc.
1001 Eastwind Drive
Suite 301
Westerville, OH 43081

Import/Export Worker

The Job   The buying and selling of raw materials and finished products between U.S. companies and companies in foreign countries are typically handled by import and export workers. Some workers handle both importing and exporting materials; others specialize in one or the other.

Import and export workers may work for firms that do only importing, only exporting, or both. Some work in the foreign trade divisions of large companies.

An *export manager* is responsible for overall management of a company's exporting activities. He or she supervises the activities of sales workers called *foreign representatives* who live and work abroad. These foreign representatives may work in a single country or travel between several countries in the course of servicing the company's customers. They also keep the company informed of any foreign political or economic conditions that might affect business. Orders from foreign customers are processed by *export sales managers,* who draw up contracts and arrange shipping details, and *export credit managers,* who review the customer's financial status and arrange credit terms.

For importing functions, a company usually employs a *support manager* to handle the purchase of foreign goods or raw materials. He or she supervises the work of *buyers,* who live and work abroad.

Companies that do not employ their own import and export workers may utilize the services of *export brokers,* who sell the companies' goods abroad for a commission, or *import merchants,* who sell products from foreign countries in this country. A company may also sell its goods to an *export commissionhouse broker.* These brokers are speculators who buy domestic goods outright and then sell them in foreign countries.

Related jobs are sales manager, wholesaler, translator, and interpreter.

Places of Employment and Working Conditions   Most import and export workers are employed in the United States. The few overseas positions usually go to those with many years of experience or a special area of expertise.

Workers employed in the United States usually work a 35- to 40-hour week; in foreign countries they are expected to adapt to local working conditions and hours. They may be exposed to extremes in climate and living conditions and may have to spend a great deal of time traveling.

Qualifications, Education, and Training   Ability to work with details, administrative talents, diplomacy, and tactfulness are necessary. Those in sales need aggressiveness and the ability to get along with people as well as adaptability for living in foreign cultures. Knowledge of a foreign language is also usually required.

Most employers require a college degree. Some will accept a liberal arts degree, but most prefer specific areas such as law, engineering, or accounting. An advanced degree in business administration is necessary for some positions.

Many employers provide training for new employees. This usually includes classroom and on-the-job training that covers U.S. laws governing foreign trade and the practices of foreign countries.

Potential and Advancement   Job opportunities in this field are expected to increase through the year 2005. Population growth and expanding foreign trade will account for a number of new job openings.

Import and export workers can advance to management and executive positions. Buyers and foreign representatives sometimes advance by going into business for themselves as export brokers or import merchants.

Income   Beginners earn starting salaries of about $16,000 a year.

Experienced workers in management-level positions average from $23,000 to $35,000, sometimes much more.

Import and export workers who are stationed overseas receive overseas incentive allowances.

Additional Sources of Information

American Association of Exporters and Importers
11 West 42d Street
New York, NY 10036

International Group
Chamber of Commerce of the United States
1615 H Street, NW
Washington, DC 20062

National Foreign Trade Council
100 East 42d Street
New York, NY 10017

Insurance Agent and Broker

The Job   Insurance agents and brokers sell insurance policies to individuals and businesses to protect against financial losses and to provide for future financial needs. They sell one or more of the three basic types of insurance: life, property-liability (casualty), and health.

An *agent* may be either the employee of an insurance company or an independent representative of one or more insurance companies. A *broker* is not under contract to a specific insurance company or companies but places policies directly with whichever company can best serve the needs of a client. Both agents and brokers spend the largest part of their time discussing insurance needs with prospective customers and designing insurance programs to fill each customer's individual needs.

Life insurance agents and brokers (life underwriters) sell policies that provide payment to survivors (beneficiaries) when the policyholder dies. A life policy can also be designed to provide retirement income, educational funds for surviving children, or other benefits.

Casualty insurance agents and brokers sell policies that protect against financial losses from such things as fire, theft, and automobile accidents. They also sell commercial and industrial insurance such as workers' compensation, product liability, and medical malpractice.

Health insurance policies offer protection against the cost of hospital and medical care as well as loss of income due to illness or injury and are sold by both life and casualty agents and brokers.

More and more agents and brokers are becoming multiline agents, offering both life and property-liability policies to their clients. Some agents and brokers also sell securities such as mutual funds and variable annuities or combine a real estate business with insurance selling. Successful insurance agents or brokers are highly self-motivated. Anyone interested in this work as a career should be aware that many beginners leave the field because they are unable to establish a large enough clientele. For those who succeed, the financial rewards are usually very good.

Related jobs are actuary, claim representative, and underwriter.

Places of Employment and Working Conditions   Insurance agents and brokers are employed throughout the country, in all locations and communities, but the largest number work in or near large population centers.

Agents and brokers are free to schedule their own working hours but often work evenings and weekends for the convenience of their clients. In addition, hours devoted to paperwork and continuing education often add up to much more than 40 hours a week.

Agents and brokers usually pay their own automobile and travel expenses. If they own and operate their own agency, they also pay clerical salaries, office rental, and operating expenses out of their own incomes.

Qualifications, Education, and Training   Agents and brokers should be enthusiastic, self-confident, and able to communicate effectively. They need initiative and sales ability to build a clientele, and must be able to work without supervision.

Many insurance companies prefer a college degree (in almost any field) but will hire high school graduates with proven ability or outstanding potential. Courses in accounting, economics, finance, business law, and insurance subjects are the most useful, whether the agent works for an insurance company or is self-employed.

New agents receive training at the agency where they will work or at the home office of the insurance company for which they work.

All states require agents and brokers to be licensed. In most states, this requires completing specified courses and passing a written examination covering state insurance laws. Insurance companies often sponsor classes to prepare their new agents for the licensing exam, while other new agents study on their own. Some trade and correspondence schools offer courses for insurance agents.

Agents and brokers who wish to succeed in this field are constantly studying to increase their skills. They take college courses and attend educational programs sponsored by their own company or by insurance organizations. The Life Underwriter Training Council awards a diploma in life insurance marketing after successful completion of the council's two-year life program. The council also sponsors a program in health insurance. Experienced agents and brokers earn the chartered life underwriter (CLU) designation by passing a series of examinations given by the American College of Bryn Mawr, Pennsylvania. Property-liability agents receive the chartered property casualty underwriter (CPCU) designation in the same way from the American Institute for Property and Liability Underwriters.

Potential and Advancement   There are approximately 439,000 part- and full-time insurance agents and brokers.

Employment of insurance agents and brokers is expected to grow through the year 2005. Although sales volume should increase rapidly as a larger proportion of the population enters the period of peak earnings and family responsibilities, the employment of agents and brokers will not necessarily grow as rapidly as sales volume. This is due to the fact that more policies will be sold to groups and by multiline agents and because more of an agent's time-consuming paperwork will be done by computer, releasing agents to spend more time in actual selling and client contact.

Promotion to positions such as sales manager in a local office or to management positions in a home office or agency is open to agents with exceptional sales ability and leadership. However, many agents who have a good client base prefer to remain in sales, and some establish their own independent agencies or brokerage firms.

Income   Most independent insurance agents and brokers usually work on a commission basis. Earnings usually increase with experience: second-year agents average $20,100 a year; third-year, $27,700; fourth-year, $30,200; and five years or more, $50,300.

Salaried insurance sales workers who are employees of an agency earn a median annual income of $26,700. Those at the bottom of the range earn $14,900 or less, while those at the top of the range earn over $58,700.

Additional Sources of Information

General occupational information about insurance agents and brokers is available from the home offices of many insurance companies. Information on state licensing requirements may be obtained from the department of insurance at any state capital. Additional sources are:

National Association of Professional Insurance Agents
400 North Washington Street
Alexandria, VA 22314

National Association of Life Underwriters
1922 F Street, NW
Washington, DC 20006

Independent Insurance Agents of America
127 South Peyton Street
Alexandria, VA 22314

Investment Manager

The Job An investment manager's function is to manage a company's or an institution's investments. Investment decisions involve such things as what to buy in the way of securities, property for investment, or other items; or what and when to sell existing holdings for maximum return on investment.

Also called financial analysts and securities analysts, these investment specialists work for banks (where they are usually officers), insurance companies, brokerage firms, and pension plan investment firms and mutual funds. They may function as trustees for institutions or individuals with large holdings or for colleges that have endowment funds to manage. Some use their expertise as financial journalists, analyzing the market for financial publications, newspapers, and magazines.

(For a detailed description of the work of people involved in this field see the job description for market analyst.)

Places of Employment and Working Conditions Investment managers work in all parts of the country but are concentrated in Boston, Chicago, New York City, and San Francisco.

The work is very time consuming since investment specialists must read constantly—newspapers, annual reports, trade publications—to keep abreast of developments and changes in the market.

Qualifications, Education, and Training
Facility in mathematics; ability to digest, analyze, and interpret large amounts of material; an inquiring mind; and good communication skills are important in this field.

A college degree in economics, political science, business administration, finance, or marketing is preferred in the investment field. Engineering or law, especially if combined with graduate work in business administration, can also provide an excellent background. Training in mathematics, statistics, and computers is becoming increasingly important.

The mark of professionalism in this field is the chartered financial analyst (CFA) degree, which is comparable to the certified public accountant (CPA) for an accountant. To earn it, the applicant must fulfill the membership requirements of one of the financial analyst societies and complete three examination programs. Five or more years of experience as a financial analyst are necessary before the third examination can be taken.

Potential and Advancement
Job opportunities will be good through the year 2005 for those with the appropriate degrees and experience.

Since this is already a high-level position in most organizations, further advancement for an investment manager would usually take the form of moving to a larger institution or organization, if he or she has achieved a reputation for accurate analysis and wise management of investments.

Income
Investment managers who work in banking or for large institutions, such as colleges, earn up to $50,000 or more a year.

The range for all top-level analysts in this field is about $25,000 to $65,000. Some with excellent reputations earn considerably more.

Additional Sources of Information

The Institute of Chartered Financial Analysts
P.O. Box 3668
Charlottesville, VA 22903

New York Stock Exchange
11 Wall Street
New York, NY 10005

Securities Industry Association
120 Broadway
New York, NY 10271

Labor Relations Specialist

The Job The field of labor relations covers the relationship between the management of a company and the company's unionized employees. Since more and more government employees are becoming unionized, specialists in the field of labor relations are now employed in government agencies as well as in private industry.

The day-to-day administration of the provisions of a union contract is usually the responsibility of a company's personnel department or, in a large company, the industrial relations department. In a small or medium-sized company, the personnel manager might handle union matters as part of his or her responsibilities, but in a large company one or more labor relations specialists are employed. Their responsibilities include handling grievances, preparing for collective bargaining sessions, and participating in contract negotiations. In some companies, labor relations specialists are also involved in accident prevention and industrial safety programs.

A labor relations specialist must stay abreast of developments in labor law and changes in wages and benefits in local companies and within the industry, and must provide constant liaison between the company and union officials. An effective labor relations specialist must be able to work with union representatives in an atmosphere of mutual respect and cooperation.

In large companies that have both union and nonunion employees, labor relations and the personnel department are part of the industrial relations department functions.

Labor relations specialists employed by government agencies perform essentially the same duties as those employed in private industry.

Labor unions do not employ many professionally trained labor relations specialists. At the company and local level, elected union officials handle all union-management matters. At national and international union headquarters, however, research and education staffs usually include specialists with degrees in industrial and labor relations, economics, or law.

Related jobs are personnel manager and employment counselor.

Places of Employment and Working Conditions
Labor relations specialists work throughout the United States, with the largest concentrations in heavily industrialized areas.

A 40-hour workweek is usual in this field, but longer hours may be necessary during contract negotiations or during periods of labor problems.

Qualifications, Education, and Training
The ability to see opposing viewpoints is important for a labor relations specialist. Integrity, a sense of fairness, and the ability to work with people of many educational levels and social backgrounds are necessary qualities. Communications skills are indispensable.

High school courses should include social studies, English, and any courses or extracurricular activities available in public speaking and debating.

Most labor relations specialists begin their careers in personnel work and move into labor relations as they gain experience. (Educational requirements for personnel workers are listed under the personnel manager job description.) Those who enter the field of labor relations directly are usually graduates of master's degree programs in industrial or labor relations or have a law degree with course work in industrial relations. Courses in labor law, collective bargaining, labor economics and history, and industrial psychology should be included in either undergraduate or graduate study.

Potential and Advancement
There are about 252,000 people working as labor relations specialists. Substantial growth is expected in this field, with the most job opportunities in private business as employers try to provide effective training and employee relations for a rapidly growing work force. In spite of this projected growth in the field, there will be competition for available job openings since there are many qualified workers and college graduates with degrees in labor relations.

Labor relations specialists who gain substantial experience and establish a widely known reputation sometimes work as federal mediators. Their services are made available to companies or industries that have arrived at a stalemate in contract negotiations with a union.

Income
The average annual salary for labor relations specialists is $29,000, with the top 10 percent earning over $52,000 and the bottom 10 percent earning less than $15,700.

Additional Sources of Information

American Society for Personnel Administration
606 North Washington Street
Alexandria, VA 22314

American Arbitration Association
140 West 51st Street
New York, NY 10020

Lawyer

The Job The basic work of a lawyer involves interpreting the law and applying it to the needs of a particular case or client.

Lawyers, also called attorneys, who have a general practice handle a variety of legal matters—making wills, settling estates, preparing property deeds, and drawing up contracts. Others specialize in criminal, corporate, labor, tax, real estate, or international law.

Most lawyers are in private practice, either alone or in a law firm. Business firms employ lawyers as salaried in-house counselors to handle company legal matters. The federal government employs lawyers in the Department of Justice and other regulatory agencies; state and local governments employ more. A few lawyers teach full- or part-time in law schools.

Many people with legal training do not practice law but instead use their legal knowledge as a background for careers in financial analysis, insurance claim adjusting, tax collection, or management consulting. Others work as parole officers or law enforcement officers. Many elected public officials also have a background in law.

Places of Employment and Working Conditions Lawyers are needed in every community and by businesses and government agencies throughout the country.

Lawyers often work long hours and are under considerable pressure when a case is being tried. Those in private practice, however, can determine their own hours and case loads and are usually able to work past the usual retirement age.

Qualifications, Education, and Training
Assertiveness, an interest in people and ideas, the ability to inspire trust and confidence, and top-notch debating and writing skills are necessary for this field. A successful lawyer must be able to research and analyze a case and to think conceptually and logically.

High school courses that develop language and verbal skills are important. Typing, American history, civics and government, and any training in debating, public speaking, or acting will prove useful.

At least seven years of full-time study beyond high school are necessary to obtain a law degree. This study includes four years of college and three years of law school. About one in six graduates attends law school on a part-time basis, taking four years or longer to complete the work.

Although there is no specific "prelaw" college program, the best undergraduate training is one that gives the student a broad educational background while developing the writing, speaking, and thinking skills necessary for a legal career. Majors in the social sciences, natural sciences, and humanities are suitable and should include courses in economics, philosophy, logic, history, and government. Good grades are very important.

Most law schools test an applicant's aptitude for the study of law by requiring the applicant to take the Law School Admission Test (LSAT). Competition for admission to law school is intense. At one point in the mid-1970s, the ratio of applicants to available openings was ten to one. Although this has slowed to some extent, stiff competition for entrance into law school will remain for the foreseeable future.

Students should attend a law school that is approved by the American Bar Association (ABA) or by an individual state. ABA approval indicates that the school meets the minimum standards of education necessary for practice in any state; state-approved law schools that lack ABA approval prepare graduates for practice in that particular state only. A few states recognize the study of law done entirely in a law office or a combination of law office and law school study. California will accept the study of law by correspondence course, if all other qualifications are met. Several states require the registration and approval of law students by the state board of examiners before they enter law school or during the early years of legal study.

The first part of law school is devoted to the study of fundamental courses such as constitutional law, contracts, property law, and judicial procedure. Specialized courses in such fields as tax, labor, or corporate law are also offered. The second part of law school consists of practical training through participation in school-sponsored legal aid activities, courtroom practice in the school's practice court under the supervision of experienced lawyers, and through writing on legal issues for the school's law journal.

Upon successful completion of law school, graduates usually receive the degree of juris doctor (J.D.) or bachelor of law (L.L.B.). Those who intend to teach, do research, or specialize usually continue with advanced study.

All states require a lawyer to be admitted to the state bar before practicing law. Requirements include a written examination, at least three years of college, and graduation from an ABA- or state-approved law school.

Potential and Advancement
There are about 633,000 lawyers practicing in the United States. Although this field is expected to grow steadily, a rapid increase in the number of law school graduates in recent years has created keen competition for available jobs. This situation will probably continue. Graduates of prestigious law schools and those who rank high in their graduating classes will have the best chance of securing salaried positions with law firms, corporations, and government agencies and as law clerks (research assistants) for judges. Lawyers who wish to establish a new practice will find the best opportunities in small towns and in expanding suburban areas.

Lawyers advance from positions as law clerks to experienced lawyers through progressively more responsible work. Many establish their own practice. After years of experience, some lawyers become judges.

Income
Lawyers who establish their own practice usually earn little more than expenses during the first few years, but their income increases rapidly as the practice develops. Private practitioners who are partners in a law firm generally earn more than those who practice alone.

Lawyers starting in private industry average about $47,000 a year, with graduates from top law schools starting at over $80,000. Starting salaries with the federal government range from $25,000 to $31,000, depending on a variety of factors, including academic record and educational background.

Experienced lawyers in private industry earn over $120,000 a year on average. Some partners in the country's top law firms average over $1 million a year.

Additional Sources of Information

Information Services
American Bar Association
750 North Lake Shore Drive
Chicago, IL 60611

Association of American Law Schools
1201 Connecticut Avenue, NW
Suite 800
Washington, DC 20036

Law School Admission Services
Box 2000
Newtown, PA 18940

Management Consultant

The Job Management consultants help managers analyze the management and operating problems of an individual organization. They recommend solutions to problems concerning the objectives, policies, and functions of the organization. They may also help with the implementation of any recommended programs.

About half of all management consultants are self-employed. The rest work in management consulting firms and for federal, state, and local governments.

Businesses and industries of all kinds use the services of management consultants, as do government agencies, nonprofit organizations, and institutions such as hospitals.

Related jobs are systems analyst, operations research analyst, industrial engineer, and office manager.

Places of Employment and Working Conditions

Management consultants are employed in all areas of the country, but primarily in metropolitan areas. Some jobs may involve temporary overseas assignment if multinational corporations are involved.

Management consultants work long hours. A 50-hour week is a short week; most consultants work even more hours. Travel plays a large part in the consultant's work; some estimates say 20 to 35 percent of a consultant's time is taken up in traveling to a client's location or between different locations of a client's organization.

Qualifications, Education, and Training

An analytical mind, good judgment, objectivity, tact, good communication skills, and the ability to work as part of a team are necessary.

High school should provide a solid college preparatory course with emphasis on mathematics, social sciences, and communication skills.

A college degree in engineering, business administration, accounting, or other related fields should be followed by graduate study in business administration or public administration. Employers prefer to hire graduates of MBA or a related master's degree program.

A number of professional societies offer examinations leading to various certifications in this field. These include certified management consultant (CMC), certified management accountant, registered professional engineer, and certified data processor.

Potential and Advancement
There are about 151,000 people engaged in management consulting, and employment of management consultants is expected to grow rapidly through the year 2005. Most job openings will occur to replace workers who change occupations or leave the labor force.

Management consultants can advance to positions as project directors and, with extensive experience, may become associates or partners in their firm. Some advance by going into business for themselves or take a high-level job with a large corporation.

Income
Salaries for management analysts and consultants vary widely by experience, education, and employer. In 1990, wage and salary workers had median annual earnings of about $39,900. The middle 50 percent earned between $28,000 and $53,100.

In the federal government, management analysts earn an average annual salary of $41,353.

Additional Sources of Information

The Council of Consulting Organizations, Inc.
251 Fifth Avenue
New York, NY 10175

Manufacturer's Sales Representative

The Job Most manufacturing firms sell their products to businesses, other industrial firms, and retail outlets through their own sales representatives. Familiarly known as *sales reps* or *manufacturer's reps,* these sales workers are thoroughly familiar with their employer's product and often provide advice and technical expertise to the customers they service.

When the product sold is highly technical, such as computers or industrial equipment, a manufacturer usually employs engineers or other technically trained people for sales. These *sales engineers* or *technical sales workers* may design systems for the client, supervise installation of equipment, and provide training for the client's employees who will use the new equipment or material.

Related jobs are sales manager, engineer, and wholesaler.

Places of Employment and Working Conditions Some
sales reps work out of local or regional offices, which keeps them fairly close to home. Others cover large territories and do a great deal of traveling. Since they almost always are at least partially compensated by commission, successful sales reps spend as much time as possible calling on customers during business hours and do any necessary traveling on evenings and weekends.

Qualifications, Education, and Training Sales skills, asser-
tiveness, a pleasant personality, physical stamina, and the ability to get along with all kinds of people are necessary for this job.

A college preparatory course should be followed in high school. Part-time or summer job experience in selling is valuable experience.

A college degree is becoming increasingly important for those who wish to work as a manufacturer's sales representative. Manufacturers of nontechnical products often prefer a liberal arts, business administration, or marketing degree. Other employers have special educational requirements: *pharmaceutical retailers* (drug sales workers) need training at a college of pharmacy; chemical manufacturers require a degree in chemistry; a computer manufacturer might hire only electronic engineers for its sales positions.

Regardless of the field, employers usually provide a training period of up to two years for new employees. Some training programs consist of classroom instruction plus on-the-job training in a branch office under the supervision of a field sales manager. In other programs, trainees are rotated through a number of jobs and departments to learn all phases of production, installation, and service of the employer's product before being assigned to a sales territory.

Potential and Advancement

There are about 642,000 manufacturers' sales representatives. The employment outlook for this field is good through the year 2005, as the demand for more and more products will increase the demand for trained sales workers. Employers are expected to be very selective, however, and those with solid educational backgrounds will get the choice jobs.

Experienced and hard-working people in this field can advance to branch manager and district manager positions and to executive-level positions such as sales manager. Many of the top-level corporate positions in industry are filled by people who started out in sales positions.

Income

Manufacturers' sales representatives may be paid in a number of ways—a salary (usually for trainees), salary plus commission, or straight commission. Many companies also provide bonuses based on sales performance.

Earnings for beginning sales reps range from about $23,000 to $28,000 a year. The highest starting salaries are paid by manufacturers of electrical and electronics equipment, construction materials and tools, food products, rubber goods, and scientific and precision instruments.

Experienced sales reps have median annual earnings of $31,000 a year; some earn more than $59,000 a year.

Additional Sources of Information

Sales and Marketing Executives International
Statler Office Towers #458
Cleveland, OH 44115

Manufacturers' Agents National Association
23016 Mill Creek Road
P.O. Box 3467
Laguna Hills, CA 92654

National Association of Wholesalers-Distributors
1725 K Street, NW
Suite 710
Washington, DC 20006

Market Analyst

The Job   The decision to buy, hold, or sell securities is sometimes made by utilizing the knowledge of the individual buyer or seller, but most individuals consult their stockbroker for advice. The stockbroker, in turn, depends on the expertise of the research department of his or her firm to provide the necessary information. These experts are called market analysts or securities analysts.

In addition to being employed in brokerage houses, market analysts and securities analysts are also employed by investment banking firms, bank trust departments, insurance companies, pension and mutual funds, investment advisory firms, and institutions such as colleges that have endowment funds to manage. All these organizations expect the same thing: expert advice that will help them to invest wisely with the best return on their money.

Market analysts evaluate the market as a whole. They study information on changes in the gross national product, cost of living, personal income, rate of employment, construction starts, fiscal plans of the federal government, growth and inflation rates, balance of payments, market trends, and indexes of common stocks. They also monitor events that might produce a psychological reaction in the market: international crisis, political activity, or a tragedy large enough to cause the market to change direction. Market analysts also keep an eye on business and industry developments and actions of the Federal Reserve to loosen or tighten credit.

Securities analysts study and analyze individual companies or industries, relating knowledge of the current and future state of the economy to predict the future performance of the company or industry. Analysts may specialize in a specific area such as companies involved in energy production or the aircraft-manufacturing industry. The analyst studies all available material on an individual company, including annual reports and details of company management, and sometimes travels to the company to take a closer look in person.

An investor who has an investment portfolio containing a number of different securities needs advice not only on the individual securities but also on the makeup of the entire portfolio. A *portfolio analyst* has the broad general knowledge to give advice on the market and its relationship to the objectives of the investor. The accumulation of a balanced portfolio can then be accomplished.

Those analysts who deal in securities actually combine elements of all of these three areas within the scope of their work. But in organizations that employ large numbers of researchers, the jobs are often separate.

Related jobs are actuary, economist, insurance agent and broker, investment manager, statistician, securities sales worker, and stockbroker.

Places of Employment and Working Conditions Analysts

work in all parts of the country but are concentrated in Boston, Chicago, New York City, and San Francisco. Major brokerage houses have branch offices in about 800 cities.

Analysts find their work fascinating but time consuming. They must read constantly—newspapers, annual reports, trade publications—to keep abreast of developments and changes in the market. Their advancement depends on the reputation they achieve for accurate analysis and predictions. They are sometimes required to make decisions quickly on securities worth thousands, or even millions, of dollars.

Qualifications, Education, and Training The ability to inter-

pret and analyze large amounts of material, an inquiring mind, and facility in mathematics are absolutely necessary. Good communication skills are also important.

A high school background with plenty of mathematics and preparation for college is essential. Some type of selling experience is usually necessary.

A college degree is required by just about all employers. Economics, political science, and business administration are the preferred degrees. Engineering, law, finance, and marketing, especially when combined with graduate work in business administration, are also accepted. The growing use of computers in this field often requires the addition to research staffs of those trained in mathematics and statistics.

The mark of professionalism among analysts is the chartered financial analyst (CFA) degree, comparable to the CPA for an accountant. To earn this degree, an analyst must fulfill the membership requirements of one of the financial analyst societies in the United States and complete three examination programs. Analysts must have five or more years of experience before taking the third examination.

Potential and Advancement Job opportunities in this field will be

good through the year 2005 for those with appropriate degrees and some knowledge of computers.

In the securities field, research departments are considered the best springboard to advancement, since analysts acquire in-depth knowledge of the economy and the market. Within research, the career path is usually junior analyst; analyst, sometimes in a specialty field; then senior analyst. Advancement to management positions in branch offices is also possible.

Income Beginning analysts with an MBA earn $22,000 a year; experi-

enced analysts, about $35,000.

Senior analysts who acquire a reputation can earn over $100,000 a year.

Additional Sources of Information

The Institute of Chartered Financial Analysts
P.O. Box 3668
Charlottesville, VA 22903

New York Stock Exchange
11 Wall Street
New York, NY 10005

Securities Industry Association
120 Broadway
New York, NY 10271

Marketing Researcher

The Job   Marketing researchers plan and design research projects, conduct interviews and other fact-gathering operations, and tabulate and analyze the resulting material.

The information a marketing researcher provides may help a company to decide on brand names, product and packaging design, company locations, and the type of advertising to use.

A *marketing research director* designs a research project after studying a company's sales records, its competitors, and the consumer market that uses the type of product or service the company offers. He or she then calls on members of the marketing research staff to implement the project.

A *statistician* will determine a sample group of consumers to be studied. A *senior analyst* or *project director* might design a questionnaire or a mail or telephone survey for field interviewers to use. *Coders* and *tabulators* synthesize the results, which are reviewed by a *research analyst*, who studies the results and makes recommendations based on the findings.

Advertising researchers specialize in studying the effects of advertising. They pretest commercials, test-market new products, and analyze the appropriateness of the various media (radio, television, newspapers, magazines, or direct mail) for a particular product or advertiser. Beginners in this field start by coding and tabulating data. They move on to interviewing and writing reports and may move up to jobs as research assistants as they gain experience.

Many opportunities for part-time work exist in marketing research. Coding, tabulating, interviewing, and making telephone surveys are jobs for which research organizations often hire people who can work odd hours or during peak work loads. High school and college students and people who work at home will find this a good field for summer jobs or for weekend or evening work.

Related jobs are advertising account executive, advertising manager, advertising worker, mathematician, statistician, and psychologist.

Places of Employment and Working Conditions   Most market researchers are employed by manufacturers, advertising agencies, and market research firms. The largest corporations are in Chicago, New York City, and Washington, DC, but job opportunities exist in almost every large city.

The usual workweek is 40 hours, but those conducting interviews and surveys are likely to have evening and weekend work. Market researchers often work under pressure and may be called upon to work overtime to meet deadlines. Although this is basically an office job, travel is a necessary part of the work in the information-gathering stages. The travel may be local or far afield depending on the scope and design of the research project.

Qualifications, Education, and Training   Assertiveness, analyzing skills, and communication skills are very important.

High school courses should include English, mathematics, and public speaking. Summer or part-time jobs coding or taking surveys are good experience.

A college degree is required for just about all of the full-time jobs in marketing research. A bachelor's degree in liberal arts, business administration, marketing, economics, or mathematics is necessary for most trainee positions. Courses in English, marketing economics, statistics, psychology, sociology, and political science should be included. A knowledge of data processing is of increasing importance as the use of computers for sales forecasting, distribution, and cost analysis is growing.

Advanced degrees are becoming more and more important for jobs beyond the entry level and for promotion. Job applicants with a combination background—for example, a bachelor's degree in statistics and a master's degree in marketing or business administration—have a good chance of being hired at the management level right out of college. Industrial marketing firms prefer those with a bachelor's degree in a related field, such as engineering, plus a master's degree in a marketing-related field.

Potential and Advancement   There are about 37,000 marketing researchers and thousands more who work part-time taking surveys and interviewing consumers. Job opportunities will be good in this field, as the growth in population and continued emphasis on advertising will result in more marketing jobs. Those with advanced degrees will be the most in demand.

Promotion is slower in this field than in most others requiring similar training; the pay scale for beginners, however, is better than that in many fields. Once a marketing research worker reaches the research assistant level, promotion is possible to junior analyst, then to senior analyst or project director. Top jobs, such as marketing research director, are few and require many years of experience plus good management skills.

Many experienced marketing researchers go into business for themselves, doing independent marketing surveys or acting as marketing consultants.

Income   According to a 1990 survey by the College Placement Council, persons with a bachelor's degree in economics received an average starting salary of about $25,200 a year; in marketing, about $23,500.

Median annual earnings of full-time economists were about $35,800 in 1990.

The median base salary of business economists in 1990 was $60,000, according to a survey by the National Association of Business Economists.

Additional Sources of Information

American Marketing Association
250 South Wacker Drive
Suite 200
Chicago, IL 60606

Marketing Research Association
2189 Silas Deone Highway
Suite 5
Rocky Hill, CT 06067

Office Manager

The Job   The title *office manager* brings to mind the secretary or clerk who has worked her or his way up in the office hierarchy to the top supervisory position. While this description is accurate to some degree, the field also includes office management positions that are much more complex and far-reaching.

In a small or medium-sized company, an office manager would supervise the day-to-day work of a clerical staff, which might include overseeing accounting functions such as billing, maintenance of personnel records, payroll, plus all other secretarial and clerical functions. The mail room, telephone switchboard, and duplicating equipment would also be part of the office manager's responsibilities. The size and makeup of the office staff would vary depending on the company and its requirements.

In a large company, the office manager is responsible for a larger and much more complex office staff, often at multiple locations within the company buildings. With one of many possible titles—director of secretarial support systems, administrative manager, office administrator—a manager at this level is involved in systems analysis and electronic data processing as well as office systems, procedures, and operations.

A rapidly growing specialty within this field is management of a centralized word processing facility within a company in which trained specialists, specific procedures, and the latest in automatic equipment are combined to handle the clerical needs of a variety of departments. Such a *word processing manager* coordinates the word processing services with the needs of the user departments and is responsible for staff levels and training, budgets, and the design and implementation of word processing systems.

The number of the clerical workers varies from organization to organization depending on the nature of the organization. The greatest concentrations of clerical workers and the managers who oversee their work are in public administration, insurance, finance, and banking. Other large employers are the wholesale and retail fields and manufacturing firms.

Related jobs are accountant, bank worker, civil service worker (federal, municipal, and state), computer programmer, industrial engineer, personnel manager, secretary, and systems analyst.

Places of Employment and Working Conditions   Although
the usual office workweek is 40 hours, office managers often put in extra hours.

The responsibilities of planning and organization, plus meetings with executives of user departments, sometimes add many hours to the daily schedule.

The entire clerical staff may work under a great deal of pressure to meet deadlines and handle busy seasons.

Qualifications, Education, and Training

A successful office manager must have a talent for organization, an analytical mind, and the ability to work with detail. Creativity, resourcefulness, flexibility, self-assurance, tact, and the ability to get along with people are also necessary. Good communication skills and a background that includes clerical skills are solid assets.

A high school student looking forward to a career in office management should take business courses as well as those courses necessary to enter college or a good business school. Part-time or summer work experience in an office is valuable preparation.

A college degree is usually necessary for a person to achieve the top levels in this field. Small businesses that require a degree often prefer a bachelor's degree in accounting, while large companies often prefer a degree in business administration. Some colleges offer a major or minor in office management.

Business schools, trade and technical schools, community colleges, and university extension programs also offer a variety of programs in this field, some leading to a degree. In addition to taking courses in office management, the student should include systems and procedures, data processing, accounting, and personnel management to acquire diversified business training. A number of two- and four-year degree programs offer electives in law or economics and other liberal arts courses to provide a well-rounded education.

Home study programs are also available for office management. The diploma awarded by such programs does not carry the prestige of a college degree, but many people find them convenient for supplementary study in specific areas of business management.

Large corporations often have training programs in office management, but these programs are usually open only to college graduates.

Regardless of educational background, people in this field continue to study throughout their careers. New developments in office technology alone would require this. In addition to taking college courses, most office managers attend seminars and conferences sponsored by various professional societies as well as training sessions and workshops presented by office equipment manufacturers.

Potential and Advancement

Qualified office managers will continue to be in demand through the year 2005. While there will continue to be a place for the skilled clerical worker who advances through the ranks, the growing complexity of the office communications and data processing functions of even small companies will require more comprehensive knowledge and training than are acquired by that route. The best job opportunities will be for those with a college degree and diversified business experience.

Office managers are already at the middle-management level. In companies where the office administration function is a major component of the firm's service, office managers can advance to top-level executive positions.

Income Salaries of office managers vary widely depending on the size of the company and its clerical staff, responsibilities, and the complexity of the job.

Median annual earnings are about $25,800, with the bottom 10 percent earning less than $15,300 and the top 10 percent more than $44,700.

Additional Sources of Information

American Management Association
135 West 50th Street
New York, NY 10020

Association of Information Systems Professionals
104 Wilmot Road
Suite 201
Deerfield, IL 60015

Administrative Management Society
4622 Street Road
Trevose, PA 19047

Operations Research Analyst

The Job An organization or system can usually be operated in several ways, but the best way is not necessarily the most obvious one. Operations research specialists use their knowledge of engineering, mathematics, and economics to decide on the most efficient way to use all available resources to achieve maximum results.

This relatively new field is concerned with the design and operation of man-machine systems. Using a number of scientific methods of analysis, operations research analysts decide on the best allocation of resources within an organization or system. These resources include such things as time, money, trained people, space, and raw materials.

In another application of operations research techniques, analysts might apply appropriate theories and methods to two possible research projects that are competing for funding. Their analysis could produce information on which project would probably achieve the best results in the shortest time with the available money and other resources.

The applications of operations research are numerous. Originated during World War II to deal with the allocation and tactical employment of available equipment, personnel, and materials, operations research is now a standard and growing aspect of management in industry, marketing, capital development, financial planning, government, and exploration activities.

A number of people in this field are engaged in teaching and research.

Related jobs are industrial engineer, systems analyst, and office manager.

Places of Employment and Working Conditions While many operations research analysts work in an office setting, many others work in classrooms, out-of-doors, and in laboratories, factories, and hospitals. It is often an active field, with the analyst moving throughout a building or to several different locations to study the operation of a company or system.

Qualifications, Education, and Training An analytical mind, resourcefulness, patience, good communication skills, and the ability to get along with people are essential.

High school should include as much mathematics and science as possible.

Employers prefer to hire graduates of master's degree programs in operations research or management science, mathematics, statistics, business administration, computer science, industrial engineering, or other quantitative disciplines. High-level computer skills have also become necessary.

Potential and Advancement There are currently about 57,000 operations research analysts. The demand for competent operations research analysts is rapidly increasing. This trend is expected to continue through 2005, providing increasing job opportunities for those who pursue it as a primary career or as an adjunct to another area of specialization.

The potential for advancement in this field is excellent. Experienced analysts can advance to supervisory and management positions in all types of organizations. Because this field provides exposure to the full spectrum of operations within a company or organization, it is becoming recognized as a major training ground for senior management and executive positions.

Many experienced operations research analysts become management consultants, opening their own companies or working for an established management consulting firm.

Income Starting salaries for operations research analysts with a master's degree were about $30,000 to $35,000 a year in 1990. Operations research analysts with experience earned about $50,000, and top salaries were more than $90,000.

In the federal government, operations research analysts averaged about $52,100 a year in 1991.

Additional Sources of Information

Education Committee
The Operations Research Society of America
428 East Preston Street
Baltimore, MD 21202

Personnel Manager

The Job Personnel managers conduct and supervise the employment functions of a company. These include recruiting, hiring, and training employees; developing wage and salary scales; administering benefit programs; complying with government labor regulations; and many other responsibilities that affect the employees.

In a small company, a personnel manager performs all these functions, usually assisted by one or two workers who help with interviewing and perform clerical duties related to the personnel department. In a large company, the personnel manager supervises a staff of trained personnel workers that includes some or all of the following specialists.

A *personnel recruiter* searches for promising job applicants through advertisements and employment agencies. A recruiter may also travel to college campuses to talk to students who are about to graduate. *Employment interviewers* talk to job applicants, sometimes administer and interpret tests, and may make some final hiring decisions.

Job analysts collect and analyze detailed information on each job within a company to prepare a description of each position. These descriptions include the duties of a particular job and the skills and training necessary to perform the job. Position descriptions are used by *salary and wage administrators* when they develop or revise pay scales for a company. They also use information gathered in surveys of wages paid by other local employers or by other companies within the same industry. Wage and salary administrators also must adhere to government regulations such as minimum wage laws.

Training specialists may supervise or conduct orientation sessions for new employees, prepare training materials and manuals, and handle in-house training programs for employees who wish to upgrade existing skills or gain promotion. In some companies, a training specialist may handle details concerning apprenticeship or management trainee programs.

An *employee benefits supervisor* provides information and counseling to employees regarding the various fringe benefits offered by a company. The supervisor is also in charge of the administration of these programs, which may include health, life, and disability insurance and pension plans. Other employee services such as cafeterias, newsletters, and recreational facilities are also covered.

Some companies now employ a special personnel worker to handle all matters pertaining to the government's equal employment opportunity regulations and the company's affirmative action programs.

Personnel workers in federal, state, and local government agencies have the added duties of devising, administering, and scoring the competitive civil service examinations that are administered to all applicants for public employment. Others oversee compliance with state and federal labor laws, health and safety regulations, and equal employment opportunity programs.

Personnel specialists also work for private employment agencies, executive search organizations, and ''office temporaries'' agencies. A few work as self-employed management consultants, and others teach at the college and university level.

Related jobs are employment counselor and labor relations specialist.

Places of Employment and Working Conditions
Job opportunities for personnel specialists and personnel managers exist throughout the country, with the largest concentrations in highly industrialized areas.

Personnel managers work in clean, comfortable offices. Most work a standard 35- to 40-hour week. While most of their time is spent in offices, some personnel workers travel to attend professional meetings and to recruit on college campuses.

Qualifications, Education, and Training
Integrity and fair-mindedness are important qualifications for those interested in personnel work, because they are often called on to act as the liaison between the company and its employees in the day-to-day administration of company policies. Personnel workers must be able to work with people of many educational levels and must have excellent written and oral communication skills.

In high school, a college preparatory course should include emphasis on English and social studies.

Some personnel workers enter the field as clerical workers in a personnel office and gain experience and expertise in one or more specialty areas over a period of time. In some small and medium-sized companies, they may advance to personnel manager positions on the basis of experience alone, but most employers require a college education even for entry-level jobs in personnel.

People in personnel work come from a variety of college majors. Some employers prefer a well-rounded liberal arts background; others want a business administration degree. A few insist on a degree in personnel administration or in industrial or labor relations. Government agencies prefer applicants who have majored in personnel administration, political science, or public administration. Any courses in the social sciences, behavioral sciences, and economics are also valuable.

Graduate study in industrial or labor relations is necessary for some top-level jobs in personnel work.

Potential and Advancement
About 456,000 people are employed in the overlapping fields of personnel and labor relations. These fields are expected to grow steadily, with the largest growth in the private sector.

Personnel workers can advance to supervisory and management positions in most companies. Those in middle-management positions in large companies can also advance to positions such as director of industrial relations.

Income
Personnel workers earn a median annual salary of about $30,000. Managers earn a median annual salary of $36,000, but salaries vary widely, ranging from under $19,000 to over $65,000.

In the federal government, salaries start at about $17,000 for people with a bachelor's degree or three years' working experience. Those with a master's degree start at $25,700, and those with a doctorate, $31,100.

Additional Sources of Information

Society for Human Resource Management
606 North Washington Street
Alexandria, VA 22314

American Society for Training and Development
1640 King Street
Box 1443
Alexandria, VA 22313

International Personnel Management Association
1617 Duke Street
Alexandria, VA 22314

Production Manager, Industrial

The Job   Production managers coordinate the activities of production departments of manufacturing firms. They are part of middle management, just below corporate, or top-level management, which sets long-range goals and policies.

Production managers carry out the plans of top management by planning and organizing the actual production of company products. They work closely with industrial designers, purchasing managers, labor relations specialists, industrial traffic managers, and production supervisors. Their responsibilities include materials control (the flow of materials and parts into the plant), production control (efficient production processes), and quality control (testing of finished products).

Places of Employment and Working Conditions   Production managers work throughout the country, with the largest concentrations in heavily industrialized areas.

Hours for production managers are often long and irregular. In addition to their regular duties, they spend a great deal of time on paperwork and meetings and are also expected to be available at all times to handle problems and emergencies.

Qualifications, Education, and Training
Strong leadership qualities and communication skills and the ability to work well under pressure are necessary.

High school should include mathematics and science courses. A college degree is required for almost all jobs at this level. In some small companies, a production supervisor (foreman) or technical worker may occasionally rise through the ranks to production manager, but he or she usually acquires some college training along the way.

Some companies will hire liberal arts graduates as production managers, but most employers prefer a bachelor's degree or advanced degree in engineering or business administration. A very effective combination is a bachelor's degree in engineering and a master's degree in business administration.

Some companies have management training programs for new graduates. As a trainee, the employee spends several years, usually in several different departments, gathering experience.

Potential and Advancement
Demand for production managers will decrease through the year 2005. Best opportunities will be for college graduates who have accumulated experience in a variety of industrial production areas.

Since this is already a high management level, it takes outstanding performance to be promoted to the corporate level; only a very few get to be vice president of manufacturing. Most production managers advance by moving to a larger company where the responsibilities are greater and more complex.

Income
Salaries vary greatly from industry to industry and also depend on size of plant. Production managers in large plants earn as much as $60,000 a year and receive bonuses based on performance.

Additional Sources of Information

American Management Association
135 West 50th Street
New York, NY 10020

American Production and Inventory Control Society
500 West Annandale Road
Falls Church, VA 22046

Public Relations Worker

The Job   Building, maintaining, and promoting the reputation and image of
an organization or a public figure constitute the work of public relations specialists. They use their skills in sales promotion, political campaigns, and many
other fields.

A large corporation employs public relations workers to present the company
in a favorable light to its various audiences—its customers, employees, stockholders, and the community where the company is located. A college or university uses its public relations staff to present an image that will attract students.
A government agency explains its work to the public by means of public relations
specialists.

Public relations workers also have the opposite duty—to keep their employers
aware of the attitudes of their various publics. For example, a public relations
specialist working for a manufacturing firm located in a city neighborhood might
advise the company that nearby residents blame the company for parking and
traffic problems in the area. Resulting company efforts to provide more employee parking facilities or to reschedule deliveries and shipments to off-peak
traffic hours would then be well publicized to improve the relations between the
company and its nearby public.

In small businesses, one person may handle all public relations functions, including writing press releases and speeches for company officials, placing information with various newspapers or radio stations, representing the employer at
public functions, or arranging public appearances for the employer. On a large
public relations staff, a *public relations manager* would be assisted by many different specialists, each handling a single phase of publicity. In some companies,
public relations functions are combined with advertising or sales promotion
work.

Many public relations specialists work for consulting firms that provide services for clients on a fee basis. Others work for nonprofit organizations, advertising agencies, and political candidates. Those who work for government agencies
are often called *public information specialists.*

Related jobs are advertising account executive, advertising manager, advertising worker, and newspaper reporter.

Places of Employment and Working Conditions   Public re-
lations specialists are found in organizations of all kinds and in all areas of the
country. Public relations consulting firms, however, are concentrated in large
metropolitan areas. Many are located in New York City, Los Angeles, Chicago,
and Washington, DC.

The usual workweek in this field is 35 to 40 hours, but attendance at meetings and community affairs can often mean overtime or evening hours. In some assignments, a public relations specialist may be on call at all times or may be required to travel for extended periods while accompanying a client such as a political candidate or other public figure.

Qualifications, Education, and Training

Self-confidence, enthusiasm, assertiveness, an outgoing personality, and imagination are necessary characteristics for success in public relations. The ability to motivate people, an understanding of human psychology, and outstanding communications skills are also necessary.

High school courses should emphasize English—especially writing skills. Any courses or extracurricular activities in public speaking or writing for school newspapers are valuable, as are summer or part-time jobs for radio or television stations or newspapers.

A college degree in journalism, communications, or public relations is the usual preparation for this field. Some employers prefer a degree in a field related to the firm's business—science, engineering, or finance, for example—plus course work or experience in public relations or communications. Some firms especially seek out college graduates who have work experience in one of the news media, which is how many writers, editors, and newspaper reporters enter the public relations field.

The Public Relations Society of America accredits public relations specialists who have worked in the field for at least five years. Applicants for this professional designation must pass a comprehensive six-hour examination that includes five hours of written and one hour of oral examination.

Job applicants in this field at all levels of experience are expected to present a portfolio of public relations projects on which they have worked.

Potential and Advancement

About 109,000 people work in public relations. Because this is a glamorous and popular field, competition for jobs is stiff. Over the long run, job opportunities are expected to increase but general economic conditions can cause temporary slow periods when companies delay expansion or cut public relations budgets. Job applicants with solid academic backgrounds plus some media experience should have the best opportunities.

Advancement usually takes the form of handling more demanding and creative assignments or transferring to a larger company. Experienced public relations specialists often start their own consulting firms.

Income   Median annual earnings for salaried public relations specialists were $30,000 in 1990. The middle 50 percent earned between $21,000 and $41,000 annually; the lowest 10 percent earned less than $15,000; and the top 10 percent earned over $52,000.

In the federal government, persons with a bachelor's degree generally started at $21,000 a year in 1991; those with a master's degree generally started at $25,700 a year. Public affairs specialists in the federal government averaged $41,500 a year in 1991.

Additional Sources of Information

Career Information
Public Relations Society of America, Inc.
33 Irving Place
New York, NY 10003

PR Reporter
P.O. Box 600
Exeter, NH 03833

Service Department
Public Relations News
127 East 80th Street
New York, NY 10021

Purchasing Agent

The Job   Purchasing agents buy the raw materials, products, and services a company needs for its operation. They coordinate their buying schedules with company production schedules so that company funds will not be tied up unnecessarily in materials ordered too soon or in too large a quantity.

In small companies, a *purchasing manager,* assisted by purchasing agents and expediters, handles all aspects of buying. Large companies employ many purchasing agents who specialize in one item or a group of related items.

Beginners in this field function as junior purchasing agents, ordering standard and catalog items until they gain enough experience to handle more difficult assignments.

Almost half of all purchasing agents work in manufacturing industries. Others are employed by government agencies, construction companies, hospitals, and schools.

Related jobs are retail buyer, traffic manager, and production manager.

Places of Employment and Working Conditions   Purchasing agents work in all sections of the country but are concentrated in heavily industrialized areas.

They usually work a standard 40-hour workweek but may have longer hours during peak production periods if they work in a seasonal industry.

Qualifications, Education, and Training   A purchasing agent must be able to analyze numbers and technical data to make responsible buying decisions. The person must have a good memory for details and be able to work independently.

High school courses should include mathematics and science; business courses are also helpful.

Small companies sometimes promote clerical workers or technicians into purchasing jobs or hire graduates of two-year colleges. Most companies, however, require at least a bachelor's degree in liberal arts or business administration with course work in purchasing, accounting, economics, and statistics. Companies that produce complex products such as chemicals or machinery may prefer a degree in science or engineering with an advanced degree in business administration.

Regardless of their educational background, beginners usually undergo an initial training period to learn the company's operating and purchasing requirements and procedures. Successful purchasing agents keep up with developments in their field through participation in seminars offered by professional societies and by taking courses at local colleges and universities.

In private industry, the recognized mark of experience and professional competence is the designation *certified purchasing manager* (CPM), conferred by the National Association of Purchasing Management, Inc. In government agencies, the designation is *certified public purchasing officer* (CPPO), which is conferred by the National Institute of Governmental Purchasing, Inc. Both have educational and experience standards and require a series of examinations.

Potential and Advancement   There are about 300,000 purchasing agents; growth in this field is expected. Job opportunities will be best for those with graduate degrees in business administration or a bachelor's degree. Graduates of two-year programs will find the best opportunities with small firms.

Purchasing agents can advance to purchasing manager and to executive positions such as director of purchasing or materials management. Some advance by moving to larger companies with more complex purchasing requirements.

Income   Median annual earnings for purchasing agents were about $26,900 in 1990. Those at the top of the pay scale earned more than $45,300, and those at the bottom, less than $16,100.

Purchasing agents in the federal government averaged $21,928 in 1990.

Additional Sources of Information

National Association of Purchasing Management, Inc.
P.O. Box 22160
Tempe, AZ 85282

National Institute of Governmental Purchasing, Inc.
1912 Woodford Road
Vienna, VA 22182

Real Estate Agent/Broker

The Job   The sale and rental of residential and commercial properties are handled by real estate agents and brokers. If they belong to the National Board of Realtors, brokers are called realtors; agents are realtor-associates. They also appraise, manage, or develop property. Some combine a real estate business with an insurance agency or law practice.

Real estate brokers employ *real estate salesworkers,* or *agents,* to show and sell properties. Most real estate businesses sell private homes and other residential property. Some specialize in commercial or industrial property or handle farms and undeveloped land.

Before a property can pass from the seller to the buyer, a title search must be made to prove that there is no doubt about the seller's right to sell the property. This "abstract of title" is performed by an *abstractor* or an abstract company. The abstract is a condensed history of the property which includes current ownership chain of title (ownership); description of the property; and, in chronological order, all transactions that affect the property. These include liens, mortgages, encumbrances, tax assessments, and other liabilities. Abstractors work for real estate firms, title insurance companies, or abstracting companies or are self-employed.

Agents obtain listings (properties to sell) by signing an agreement with the seller giving the agent and the real estate firm the right to represent the seller in disposing of the property. It is the agent's responsibility to locate a buyer by advertising and showing the property to interested people. If the buyer requests it, the real estate agent may help locate mortgage funds. In cases where the seller's asking price is higher than the buyer is willing to pay, the agent often acts as a negotiator to bring the sale to a successful conclusion. Agents also are present at the closing when the property actually changes hands.

A successful real estate agent must be well versed in all local information relative to the type of real estate sold. An agent selling houses must know local tax and utility rates and the availability of schools, shopping facilities, and public transportation. A commercial or industrial property agent must be able to provide information on taxes, marketing facilities, local zoning regulations, the available labor market, and nearby railroad and highway facilities.

Most real estate salespeople are employed in relatively small businesses. Some large real estate firms employ several hundred agents in many branch offices, but five to ten people is the usual number employed by a single real estate business. Many agents sell real estate on a part-time basis.

Brokers are independent business owners who are responsible for all business matters relating to the firm's function. Some brokers operate a one-person firm, doing all the selling themselves. A related job is real estate appraiser.

Places of Employment and Working Conditions
Real estate agents and brokers work throughout the country in communities of all sizes.

The working hours of real estate agents and brokers are irregular, and evening and weekend hours are the norm. They spend a great deal of time on the phone obtaining listings and are also responsible for the paperwork on the sales they handle.

Qualifications, Education, and Training
A pleasant personality, neat appearance, and tact are necessary qualities for a successful real estate agent. Sales ability, along with a good memory for names and faces, is also very important.

Some real estate brokers prefer to hire college graduates with a degree in real estate or business, but most will hire high school graduates with sales ability.

All states and the District of Columbia require agents and brokers to be licensed.

A college degree is not necessary to obtain a license, but most states require at least 30 hours of classroom instruction. Local colleges, adult education programs, and correspondence schools offer the courses necessary to obtain a license, and many prospective real estate agents hold down a full-time job while studying to be a real estate agent. Many brokers hire real estate students as office assistants or rent collectors while they are preparing for the state licensing exam, but others hire only those who have already obtained a license.

Some colleges and universities offer an associate's or bachelor's degree with a major in real estate; several offer advanced education courses to agents and brokers.

A prospective agent must be 18 years old, a high school graduate, and pass a written test on real estate transactions and state laws regarding the sale of real estate to complete the licensing requirements.

Candidates for a broker's license must complete 90 hours of formal training, have a specified amount (usually one to three years) of real estate selling experience, and pass a more comprehensive exam. Some states waive the experience requirements if the candidate has a bachelor's degree in real estate.

Potential and Advancement   There are about 413,000 real estate agents and brokers in the United States. The employment outlook is good through the year 2005, and beginners will find it relatively easy to find a job. But anyone entering real estate should be aware that they may not earn enough to be self-supporting when working on commission. Also, during periods of economic decline, real estate sales and the demand for agents decrease.

In large real estate firms, experienced agents can advance to sales manager or general manager. Experienced sales workers often obtain a broker's license and go into business for themselves. Others go into property management or appraising. Many successful agents prefer to continue selling because the financial rewards are very good.

Income   According to a National Association of Realtors survey, the median income of full-time real estate agents was about $19,000 a year in 1990. Real estate brokers earned an estimated median gross personal income (after expenses) of $50,000 a year. The most successful agents and brokers earn considerably more. Some firms, especially the large ones, furnish group life, health, and accident insurance.

Additional Sources of Information

National Association of Realtors
875 North Michigan Avenue
Chicago, IL 60611

Real Estate Appraiser

The Job   A real estate appraiser studies and evaluates information about a property and estimates its market value. A written appraisal is then prepared to document the findings and conclusions.

An appraisal is usually required whenever a property is sold, insured, or assessed for taxation. Mortgage lenders require an appraisal as do federal, state, and local governments when acquiring property for public use. Insurance companies require an appraisal when determining the proper amount of insurance on a property.

An appraiser must be familiar with public records and their location, be able to read blueprints and mechanical drawings, recognize good and bad construction materials, and be up-to-date on building zoning laws and government regulations. Appraisers usually specialize in one type of property such as farms, single-family dwellings, industrial sites, or apartment houses.

Appraisers often enter the field from other jobs in real estate sales or management, but more and more are entering the field directly. Those with a college education have the greatest chance of success. Beginners in appraisals usually start as appraisal assistants or trainees.

Opportunities for beginners exist in local county assessors' offices and in federal, state, and city departments. Local independent appraisers also offer part-time and full-time work to beginners and college students studying real estate appraisal.

A related job is real estate agent/broker.

Places of Employment and Working Conditions   Appraisers work throughout the country, wherever property is bought, insured, or taxed.

Much of an appraiser's time is spent away from the office inspecting properties and researching records. Independent appraisers set their own working hours but frequently work evenings and weekends to meet client deadlines. Appraisers who work in salaried positions usually have more regular working hours.

Appraisers spend varying amounts of time in travel if they evaluate property in other areas or in other countries. These appraisers are usually involved in appraising industrial and commercial property or property for investment.

Qualifications, Education, and Training
An appraiser must have the highest standards of personal integrity and honesty and should possess good written and oral communication skills. An appraiser also needs good health and stamina because this is a physically demanding job.

Many private firms, financial institutions, and government agencies will hire only appraisers who have a college degree. Many colleges and universities offer programs in real estate and in real estate appraising. Other relevant courses are economics, finance, business administration, architecture, law, and engineering.

Appraisers may obtain professional recognition by working toward designations awarded by an organization. These designations are awarded by the American Institute of Real Estate Appraisers, the Society of Real Estate Appraisers, and the American Society of Appraisers.

The federal government has required that appraisers of most types of real estate be licensed. State licensing requirements must meet federal standards, but they are permitted to be more stringent than federal standards. Work experience and a passing score on a written examination are needed for certification.

Potential and Advancement
This is a good job opportunity field because there is expected to be an increased demand for home purchases and rental units. However, real estate appraising is affected by the swings in the economy. During times when the economy is weak, the earnings of appraisers decline, and many are forced to leave the occupation.

Advancement in this field depends on experience, personal ability, and effort.

Income
Beginning real estate appraisers often work on a free-lance basis and are paid by the job. They earn about $20,000 a year. More experienced real estate appraisers earn between $35,000 and $50,000 a year.

Additional Sources of Information

Contact your local board of realtors office or state real estate commission for specific requirements in your area. Information is also available from:

American Institute of Real Estate Appraisers
875 North Michigan Avenue
Chicago, IL 60611

National Association of Realtors
875 North Michigan Avenue
Chicago, IL 60611

Retail Store Manager

The Job The manager of a retail store, whether the store is large or small, has one goal—to operate the store at a profit. To this end the manager applies years of accumulated training and experience.

Retailing is one of few remaining fields where talented and hardworking people can still advance all the way to the top regardless of education. Several career paths are possible, including sales work, merchandise and fashion buying, advertising, accounting, and personnel relations. Those who reach the level of store manager usually have experience in several of these areas.

Four major tasks are involved in the operation of a retail store: merchandising (buying and selling), store operations (staffing, shipping, and receiving), accounting, and advertising. In a small store, the manager handles all of these. The manager of a large store might handle one or two of these areas personally and assign assistant managers to supervise the others. In some stores, the manager provides overall supervision and policy making while employing four or more division heads to oversee specific functions. In chain stores, centralized buying and accounting usually relieve the individual store managers of these two responsibilities.

Related jobs are retail buyer, purchasing agent, wholesaler, advertising manager, and personnel manager.

Places of Employment and Working Conditions This is a highly competitive field, and the store manager is under constant pressure to increase the store's sales volume. Many managers work 50 or more hours a week.

Managers employed by chain stores may be required to move frequently, especially during their early years with the company.

Qualifications, Education, and Training Good judgment, tact, administrative ability, a feeling for what the public wants to buy, good communication skills, and the ability to deal with all types of people are necessary for a store manager.

High school studies should include mathematics, English, and social sciences; distributive education programs, where available, provide an excellent background. Part-time or summer jobs in retail stores are good experience.

Education requirements in this field vary greatly. Some large stores and many chain stores will accept high school graduates into the management training programs. Many larger employers require a college degree in liberal arts, marketing, accounting, or business administration. Top positions in some stores require a master's degree in business administration.

Potential and Advancement Growth in retailing is expected to accompany the growth in population, creating substantial job opportunities through the year 2005. Positions in large independent stores will be the most competitive, but entry-level jobs in retailing will be numerous.

Regardless of educational background and career path within retailing, advancement to the top positions requires years of experience and a record of success at each level. When the store-manager level is achieved, sales volume figures become the deciding factor in the manager's career. Increased sales can lead to promotion to field manager or transfer to a more desirable store in a chain store operation or the opportunity to work for a larger independent store.

Income Trainees earn between $15,000 and $19,500 a year.

Experienced store managers earn from $19,500 to $31,000 or more. Many also receive bonuses or participate in profit-sharing plans, based on store sales volume.

Additional Sources of Information

National Retail Merchants Association
100 West 31st Street
New York, NY 10001

School Administrator

The Job   School administrators have the responsibility of running the various schools and school systems in the United States. Their duties depend on whether they work at the state or local level, whether they work in a public or parochial school system or private school, and on their area of responsibility.

At the state level, a *superintendent of schools* or *director of education* oversees the functioning of the public school systems and state colleges within a state. The superintendent is responsible for setting and enforcing minimum standards for schools and teachers, administering teacher certification programs, and administering whatever state and federal funds are provided for education.

At the local level, a superintendent of schools is appointed by a local public school board or by a parochial school system to administer an individual school system. The system may consist of just a few schools or many schools. The superintendent hires and supervises all personnel; prepares the school budget; is responsible for physical maintenance of buildings and equipment; makes projections for future needs; and oversees curriculum and textbook decisions, purchasing, public transportation, and many other details. The superintendent's job is often a thankless one—with the local school board and citizens, on one hand, trying to keep taxes down, and teachers trying to provide the best education possible for the students, on the other. It is the superintendent who must work to appease both groups.

The superintendent is usually assisted by various other administrators who handle special areas. *Special-subject supervisors* coordinate the activities and curriculum of a specific subject area throughout all the schools in the system. The most common special areas are music, art, remedial reading, physical education, libraries, and business or technical education. *Special-education supervisors* plan and supervise the instruction of handicapped students and, in school systems that provide them, handle programs for gifted students as well.

A *curriculum director* evaluates the subjects and activities included in the curricula of the schools within the school system and makes recommendations to teachers and other administrators.

Within an individual school, the *principal* is responsible for the day-to-day operation of the school. The principal must operate within a budget, be both an educator and a business manager, develop and maintain a good working relationship with teachers and students, handle discipline, and also oversee building maintenance.

In a private school, the principal is often called a *headmaster* or *headmistress*. If the school also provides residence facilities for its students, the headmaster has additional responsibilities besides those of a school principal. Living quarters, food, laundry, and recreation facilities and "substitute parent" functions would then be part of the headmaster's duties as well.

Places of Employment and Working Conditions
School administrators function under constant pressure, especially at the highest levels. Frustration is often part of the job, and administrators must face the fact that they are often resented by the very people they work to serve.

Hours for most administrators are long and irregular. Evening meetings and civic functions often push the total up to 50 or 60 hours or more a week.

Qualifications, Education, and Training
An interest in the development of children, the ability to get along with people, communication and business skills, patience, tact, and good judgment are all necessary.

The first step in this career field is a degree in teaching or education. Graduate study in educational administration is necessary for most administrative positions. A master's degree is the minimum requirement; top-level positions in large schools or school systems usually require a Ph.D.

Potential and Advancement
There are about 348,000 school administrators at the present time. This field is expected to grow about as fast as the average through the year 2005. There will be stiff competition for jobs in this field. Those persons who combine the appropriate educational credentials with wide experience will have the best chance of securing the choice jobs at all levels.

Income
Average annual salaries for principals in 1990-91 were: elementary, $51,500; junior high and middle school, $55,100; and senior high school, $59,100. Average annual salaries for assistant principals in 1990-91 were: elementary, $43,500; junior high and middle school, $47,000; and senior high school, $49,000.

Additional Sources of Information

American Association of School Administrators
1801 North Moore Street
Arlington, VA 22209

The National Association of Elementary School Principals
1615 Duke Street
Alexandria, VA 22314

The National Association of Secondary School Principals
1904 Association Drive
Reston, VA 22091

Securities Sales Worker (Stockbroker)

The Job When investors buy or sell stocks, bonds, or shares in mutual funds, they use the services of securities sales workers. These workers are also known as registered representatives, account executives, or customers' brokers.

Securities sales workers relay the customer's "buy" or "sell" orders to the floor of the appropriate securities exchange or to the firm's trading department and notify the customer of the completed transaction and final price. They also provide related services such as financial counseling, the latest stock and bond quotations, and information on financial positions of corporations whose securities are being traded.

Securities sales workers can help a client accumulate a financial portfolio of securities, life insurance, and other investments geared either to long-term goals such as capital growth or income or to short-term goals. Some sales workers specialize in one type of customer such as institutional investors or in certain types of securities such as mutual funds.

Beginners in this field spend much of their time searching for new customers. As they establish a clientele, they spend more time servicing their existing customers and less in seeking new ones.

Securities sales workers are employed by brokerage firms, investment banks, and mutual fund firms. Most work for a few large firms that have offices in cities throughout the country.

Places of Employment and Working Conditions Securities
sales workers are employed in cities throughout the United States, usually in the branch offices of a few large firms.

Sales workers usually work in bustling, sometimes noisy offices. Beginners usually put in long hours until they acquire a clientele, and sales workers occasionally meet with clients on evenings or weekends.

Many sales workers leave the field each year because they are unable to establish a large enough clientele.

Qualifications, Education, and Training   Selling skills and ambition are necessary for success as a securities sales worker. A sales worker should also be mature, well groomed, and able to motivate people. Many employers prefer to hire applicants who have had previous experience in sales or management positions.

A college education is preferred by the larger firms. A liberal arts background with training in economics, prelaw, business administration, or finance is particularly helpful.

Most employers provide training to new sales workers to help them meet state licensing and registration requirements. In firms that are members of major exchanges, the training program lasts at least four months. In small firms and mutual funds and insurance companies, training is shorter and less formal.

Almost all states require securities sales workers to be licensed. Licensing requirements usually include a written examination and the furnishing of a personal bond. Those who intend to sell insurance in addition to securities must be licensed for that also.

Sales workers must be registered as representatives of the firm for which they work. To qualify, they must pass the General Securities Registered Representative Examination, administered by the National Association of Securities Dealers, Inc.

Potential and Advancement   There are about 191,000 securities sales workers. Job opportunities should be favorable as employment is expected to grow substantially through the year 2005. Well-rounded, mature people with a college education and successful work experience in sales or management will be most in demand.

Securities sales workers advance primarily by increasing the number of accounts they manage. They may also handle larger accounts as they gain experience. Some advance to become branch office managers, who supervise others while managing their own accounts. A few workers advance to top management positions or become partners in their firms.

Income   According to the Securities Industry Association, average annual earnings of beginning securities sales representatives were $28,000 in 1990. Earnings of full-time, experienced securities sales representatives who served

individual investors averaged about $79,000 a year, while the relatively small number of sales representatives who handled institutional accounts averaged about $166,000.

Trainees usually are paid a salary until they meet licensing and registration requirements. After registration, a few firms continue to pay a salary until the new representative's commissions increase to a stated amount. The salaries paid during training usually range from $1,200 to $1,500 a month.

Additional Sources of Information

New York Stock Exchange
11 Wall Street
New York, NY 10005

Securities Industry Association
120 Broadway
New York, NY 10271

Systems Analyst

The Job   Systems analysts decide what new data need to be collected, the equipment needed to process the data, and the procedure to be followed in using the information within any given computer system. They use techniques such as cost accounting, sampling, and mathematical model building to analyze a problem and devise a new system to solve it.

Once a system has been developed, the systems analyst prepares charts and diagrams that describe the system's operation in terms that the manager or customer who will use the system can understand. The analyst may also prepare a cost-benefit analysis of the newly developed system. If the system is accepted, the systems analyst then translates the logical requirements of the system into the capabilities of the particular computer machinery (hardware) in use and prepares specifications for programmers to follow. The systems analyst will also work with the programmers to "debug" (eliminate errors from) a new system.

Because the work is complex and varied, systems analysts specialize in either business or scientific and engineering applications. Some analysts improve systems already in use or adapt existing systems to handle additional types of data.

Those involved in research, called *advanced systems designers,* devise new methods of analysis.

Most systems analysts are employed by banks, insurance companies, large manufacturing firms, and data processing services. Others work for wholesale and retail businesses and government agencies.

In many industries, systems analysts begin as computer programmers and are promoted to analyst positions only after gaining experience. In large data processing departments, they may start as junior systems analysts. Many persons enter this occupation after experience in accounting, economics, or business management (for business positions) or engineering (for scientific work).

Places of Employment and Working Conditions Job opportunities for systems analysts are mainly concentrated in urban areas, although opportunities exist throughout the entire country.

Systems analysts usually work a normal 40-hour week with occasional evening or weekend work.

Qualifications, Education, and Training Systems analysts must be able to think logically, to concentrate, and to handle abstract ideas. They must be able to communicate effectively with technical personnel such as programmers as well as with those who have no computer background.

High school should include as many mathematics courses as possible.

Because job requirements vary so greatly, there is no universally accepted way of preparing for a career as a systems analyst. A background in accounting, business administration, or economics is preferred by employers in business. Courses in computer concepts, systems analysis, and data retrieval techniques are good preparation for any systems analyst.

Many employers require a college degree in computer science, information science, or data processing. Scientifically oriented organizations often require graduate work as well in some combination of computer science and a science or engineering specialty.

Because technological advances in the computer field come so rapidly, systems analysts must continue their technical education throughout their careers. This training usually takes the form of one- and two-week courses offered by employers, computer manufacturers, and also software (computer systems) vendors.

The Institute for Certification of Computer Professionals confers the designation *certified data processor* (CDP) and *certified systems professional* on systems analysts who have five years of experience and who successfully complete a general examination plus exams in two specialty areas.

Potential and Advancement

There are about 463,000 systems analysts. This job field is expected to grow steadily because of the expanding use of computers. College graduates who have had courses in computer programming, systems analysis, and data processing will have the best opportunities, while those without a degree may face some competition for the available jobs that don't require a degree.

Systems analysts can advance to jobs as lead systems analysts or managers of systems analysis or data processing departments.

Income

Median annual earnings of systems analysts who worked full-time in 1990 were about $38,700. The middle 50 percent earned between $30,900 and $50,700 a year. The lowest 10 percent earned less than $23,000; the highest tenth, more than $62,400.

In the federal government, the entrance salary for recent college graduates with a bachelor's degree was about $17,000 a year in 1991.

Additional Sources of Information

Association for Systems Management
24587 Bagley Road
Cleveland, OH 44138

Institute for Certification of Computer Professionals
2200 East Devon Avenue
Suite 268
Des Plaines, IL 60018

Traffic Manager, Industrial

The Job

The efficient movement of materials into and finished products out of an industrial firm is the responsibility of an industrial traffic manager.

In the course of their work, traffic managers analyze various transportation possibilities—rail, air, truck, or water—and select the method most suited to the company's needs. They select the carrier and the route; prepare necessary shipping documents; handle claims for lost or damaged shipments; consult company officials about purchasing, producing, and scheduling shipments; and sometimes appear before rate-making and government regulatory agencies to represent their company.

Because many aspects of transportation are subject to federal, state, and local government regulations, industrial traffic managers must be well versed in all such regulations and any other legal matters that affect the shipping operations of their company. They must also be informed about advances in transportation technology and the present and future prices and availability of fuels necessary for the company's transportation requirements. Traffic managers often make decisions on or advise top management about the advisability of purchasing versus contracting for railcars or trucking fleets.

Most traffic managers work for manufacturing firms. A substantial number are employed by wholesalers, large retail stores, and chain stores.

Places of Employment and Working Conditions   Industrial traffic managers usually have standard working hours but may put in some extra time on paperwork, meetings, or travel to hearings before state and federal regulatory bodies.

Qualifications, Education, and Training   The ability to work independently, to analyze technical and numerical data, and to present facts and figures in a logical and convincing manner are all necessary for a traffic manager.

The high school curriculum should include mathematics courses.

Although some traffic managers arrive at their positions through experience only, college training is becoming more and more important in this field. Traffic managers who argue cases before the Interstate Commerce Commission, for instance, must have at least two years of college education.

Some employers prefer to hire graduates of trade or technical schools or two-year college programs in traffic management. Other employers require a college degree with a major or course work in transportation, logistics, physical distribution, business administration, economics, statistics, marketing, computer science, or commercial law.

Potential and Advancement   This relatively small field is expected to have steady growth through the year 2005, with first consideration for job openings going to college graduates with a major in traffic management or transportation.

Industrial traffic workers can advance to supervisory positions and to assistant traffic manager and traffic manager positions. Experienced industrial traffic managers very often advance by moving to a larger company where job responsibilities are more complex.

Income   Beginners in traffic management start at about $25,000 a year.

Salaries of experienced industrial traffic managers vary widely depending on the size of the company, but average about $38,000 a year.

Additional Sources of Information

American Association of State Highway and Transportation Officials
444 North Capitol
Washington, DC 20001

Institute of Transportation Engineers
525 School Street, SW
Washington, DC 20024

Travel Agent

The Job   Travel agents are specialists who make the best possible travel arrangements to fit the requirements and budgets of individuals or groups traveling anywhere in the world. A travel agent can provide a client with plane tickets and a hotel reservation or can plan a trip down to the last detail—guided tours, rental car, passports and visas, currency exchange rates.

Many services of a travel agency are provided free of charge to the customer with a service fee charged only for complicated travel and lodging arrangements.

Although personal travel experience is part of a successful agent's background, travel agents do not spend most of their time traveling and vacationing. They are usually found behind a desk talking to a customer or completing necessary paperwork or on the phone making airline, ship, or hotel reservations. Agents also speak to social and special interest groups—often presenting slide or movie presentations of vacation tours—or meet with business executives to plan company-sponsored trips and business travel.

Some large companies whose employees do a great deal of traveling employ travel agents in-house to make all the company's travel arrangements.

Places of Employment and Working Conditions Travel agents work throughout the country, but most jobs are in urban areas.

Qualifications, Education, and Training A travel agent is basically a sales representative and, as such, should have patience and a pleasant personality, enjoy dealing with the public, and be willing to work with the hard-to-please customer as well as the timid or inexperienced traveler.

Formal training is becoming more important for travel agents, as few travel agencies offer on-the-job training. Vocational schools offer training programs lasting three to twelve weeks full-time, and travel courses are offered in adult education programs and in community and four-year colleges. A few colleges offer bachelor's and master's degrees in travel and tourism. Home-study and correspondence courses are also available.

Licensing of travel agents is required in Rhode Island, and Ohio, Hawaii, and California require registration. In California, agents not approved by a corporation must have a license.

Travel experience is another important qualification for a travel agent. This is an asset when applying for a job in this field but can also be acquired during the years of training. Being able to speak from personal experience, an agent can provide more comprehensive advice to clients.

Part-time or summer jobs as a receptionist or reservation clerk in a travel agency or experience as an airline ticket clerk can provide valuable experience.

Some agencies prefer to hire college graduates, and courses in geography, foreign languages, or history are helpful. Accounting and business management are important to those who intend to open their own agencies.

Potential and Advancement There are about 132,000 travel agents. Even though the travel industry is expected to expand rapidly, competition for job openings will be tight for some positions.

Spending on travel is expected to increase significantly through the year 2005. Rising incomes and increased leisure time mean more people traveling more often than in the past. More efficient planes and economical group tour packages have brought even international travel within the budget of more Americans than ever. In addition, increased business travel, much of it international, and an increasing flow of foreign visitors to the United States will add to the demand for travel agents.

The travel industry, however, is sensitive to fluctuations in the economy. The price and availability of gasoline also have an effect on the travel industry because rapidly rising fuel costs could make a significant difference in the price of travel.

Travel agents in larger agencies can be promoted to supervisory or management positions. Some agents advance by opening their own agencies.

Income Experience, sales ability, and the size and location of the agency determine the salary of a travel agent. According to a survey conducted for *Travel Weekly* magazine, salaries of travel agents generally ranged from $12,056 for beginners to $21,715 a year for experienced agents in 1990. Salaried agents usually have standard benefits—insurance coverage, paid vacations—that self-employed agents must provide for themselves.

Earnings of self-employed travel agents depend mainly upon commissions from airlines and other carriers, tour operators, and hotels and resorts. Commissions for domestic travel arrangements are about 10 percent; and international travel, 11 percent. Travel agents must receive conference approval before they can receive commissions, however. (Conferences are organizations of shiplines, rail lines or airlines—such as the International Air Transport Association.) To obtain conference approval, the travel agency must demonstrate that it is in operation, that it is financially sound, and that it employs at least one experienced travel agent who can arrange foreign and domestic travel as well as hotel and resort accommodations. Obtaining conference approval usually takes up to a year or more, which means that self-employed agents make very little money during their first year except for hotel and tour operation commissions.

Additional Sources of Information

American Society of Travel Agents
1101 King Street
Alexandria, VA 22314

Underwriter

The Job Because insurance companies assume millions of dollars in risks by transferring the chance of loss from their policyholders to themselves, they employ underwriters to study and select the risks the company will insure. Underwriters analyze insurance applications, medical reports, actuarial studies, and other material. They must use personal judgment in making decisions that could cause their company to lose business to competitors (if they are too conservative) or to pay too many claims (if they are too liberal).

Most underwriters specialize in one of the three basic types of insurance: life, property and casualty, or health. Property and casualty underwriters also specialize by type of risk: fire, automobile, or workers' compensation, for example. Underwriters correspond with policyholders, insurance agents, and insurance office managers. They sometimes accompany salespeople as they call on customers and may attend meetings with union representatives or union members to explain the provisions of group policies.

Underwriters who specialize in commercial underwriting often evaluate a firm's entire operation before approving its application for insurance. The growing trend toward "package" underwriting of various types of risks under a single policy requires that the underwriter be familiar with several different lines of insurance rather than be specialized in just one line.

Beginners work under the close supervision of an experienced underwriter. They progress from evaluating routine applications to handling those that are more complex and have greater face value.

Related jobs are actuary, claim representative, and insurance agent and broker.

Places of Employment and Working Conditions   Most underwriters are employed in the home offices of their companies, which are usually located in and around Boston, Chicago, Dallas, Hartford, New York City, Philadelphia, San Francisco, and Des Moines. Some are also employed in regional offices in other parts of the country.

Underwriting is basically a desk job. The average workweek is 35 to 40 hours, with occasional overtime required.

Qualifications, Education, and Training   A career as an underwriter can be very satisfying to someone who likes to work with details and who enjoys relating and evaluating information. Underwriters must be able to make decisions and communicate well. They must also be imaginative and aggressive when searching out information from outside sources.

High school courses in mathematics are valuable.

Some small insurance companies will hire underwriter trainees without a college degree. Large insurance companies require a college degree, preferably in finance or business administration.

As in all jobs in the insurance industry, great emphasis is placed on the completion of independent study programs throughout an employee's career. Salary increases and tuition costs are often provided by the company on completion of a course. The study programs are available through a number of insurance organizations and professional societies.

Potential and Advancement   About 105,000 underwriters work for insurance companies at the present time. The field is expected to grow at a moderate rate.

Experienced underwriters can advance to senior or chief underwriter or to underwriting manager if they complete appropriate courses. Some are promoted to supervisory and senior management positions.

Income   According to a survey conducted by the Alliance of American Insurers in collaboration with the American Insurance Association and the National Association of Independent Insurers, personal lines underwriters earn entry-level salaries of $23,900 a year; senior level underwriters, $36,500; and managers, $54,100. Commercial lines underwriters earn entry-level salaries of $25,400 a year; senior-level underwriters, $37,200; and managers, $54,300.

Most insurance companies have liberal vacation policies and other employee benefits. Almost all insurance companies provide employer-financed group life and retirement plans.

Additional Sources of Information

American Council of Life Insurance
1001 Pennsylvania Avenue, NW
Washington, DC 20004

Insurance Information Institute
110 William Street
New York, NY 10038

Alliance of American Insurers
1501 Woodfield Road
Suite 400 W.
Schaumburg, IL 60173

The National Association of Independent Insurers
Public Relations Department
2600 River Road
Suite 845
Des Plaines, IL 60018

Wholesaler

The Job   The wholesaler is a middle link in the distribution chain between the producer of goods and the retail store in which the goods are sold. Because no producer could possibly contact all the retail outlets or industries that use his or her products and no retail store manager has the time to contact all of his or her suppliers individually, the wholesaler provides a valuable service to both segments of the marketplace.

The largest number of wholesalers, are *merchant wholesalers*, who buy merchandise outright, warehouse the merchandise until needed, and then sell to retail outlets. They employ salespeople to call on retail customers, extend credit to customers, and lend money to suppliers in the form of prepaid orders.

The second largest group in wholesaling is *manufacturer's agents*. These are independent businesspeople who contract with a manufacturer to sell a specific product or group of products, usually in a specific geographic area. A manufacturer's agent usually represents several manufacturers and sells to retail stores, local distributors, industrial concerns, and institutions. If the business is large enough, the agent may employ additional sales personnel. An industrial distributor is a wholesaler who handles the products from only one manufacturer.

Merchandise brokers may represent either the buyer or seller in a wholesale transaction. The broker, however, does not buy or take direct responsibility for the goods being sold but acts as the agent of either the buyer or seller. Merchandise brokers work mainly in a few fields—food and grocery specialties, fresh fruits and vegetables, piece goods, cotton, grain, livestock, and petroleum products.

Commission merchants usually deal in agricultural products. They take possession of, but not title to, the merchandise. They may store it, transport it, and condition it for market (inspect, weigh, grade) before finding a buyer. They charge a commission for their services as a part of the final selling price.

Auction companies are wholesalers who sell a client's product at a public auction. Most sales of this nature are in tobacco, fresh fruits and vegetables, livestock, floor coverings, furs and skins, jewelry, and furniture.

Related jobs are retail buyer, auctioneer, retail store manager, manufacturer's sales representative, and sales manager.

Places of Employment and Working Conditions   Some
wholesalers, especially the largest and best known, are in large cities such as

Chicago, Kansas City, Los Angeles, New York, and St. Louis. The others are located throughout the United States, many of them in small cities and towns.

Wholesalers, especially those dealing in perishable or seasonal goods, run the risk of sudden financial loss. They must have a secure financial base to carry them over lean periods or unexpected losses.

Qualifications, Education, and Training Good judgment, business and management skills, experience as a buyer or salesperson, and an ability to deal with people are all necessary.

There are no specific education requirements for this field. The largest wholesalers, however, usually require experience or training in business administration, sales and marketing, retailing, or a particular technical area such as electrical products or other industrial fields.

Potential and Advancement The best job opportunities for beginners are with smaller wholesalers, while persons with appropriate college education can often start in management-level positions with large wholesalers.

Income Income varies greatly depending on the size of the business. Small wholesalers earn from $12,600 to $57,000 a year; large ones earn up to $100,000.

Manufacturer's agents average about $23,000 to $67,000 a year; a few earn over $100,000.

Additional Sources of Information

National Association of Wholesaler-Distributors
1725 K Street, NW
Washington, DC 20006

Manufacturer's Agents' National Association
23016 Mill Creek Road
P.O. Box 3467
Laguna Hills, CA 92653

National-American Wholesale Grocers Association
51 Madison Avenue
New York, NY 10010

Resumes, Application Forms, Cover Letters, and Interviews

You might imagine a hurdle to leap over, or a hoop to jump through. Or a barrier to knock down. That is how many people think of resumes, application forms, cover letters, and interviews. But you do not have to think of them that way. They are not ways to keep you from a job; they are ways for you to show an employer what you know and what you can do. After all, you are going to get a job. It is just a question of which one.

Employers want to hire people who can do the job. To learn who these people are, they use resumes, application forms, written tests, performance tests, medical examinations, and interviews. You can use each of these different evaluation procedures to your advantage. You might not be able to make a silk purse out of a sow's ear, but at least you can show what a good ear you have.

Creating Effective Resumes and Application Forms

Resumes and application forms are two ways to achieve the same goal: To give the employer written evidence of your qualifications. When creating a resume or completing an application form, you need two different kinds of information: facts about yourself and facts about the job you want. With this information in hand, you can present the facts about yourself in terms of the job. You have more freedom with a resume—you can put your best points first and avoid

This article is reprinted from *Occupational Outlook Quarterly,* spring 1987, volume 31, number 1, pp. 17–23, written by Neale Baxter.

blanks. But, even on application forms, you can describe your qualifications in terms of the job's duties.

Know thyself

Begin by assembling information about yourself. Some items appear on virtually every resume or application form, including the following:

◇ Current address and phone number—if you are rarely at home during business hours, use an answering machine or try to give the phone number of a friend or relative who will take messages for you.

◇ Job sought or career goal.

◇ Experience (paid and volunteer)—date of employment, name and full address of the employer, job title, starting and finishing salary, and reason for leaving (moving, returning to school, and seeking a better position are among the readily accepted reasons).

◇ Education—the school's name, the city in which it is located, the years you attended it, the diploma or certificate you earned, and the course of studies you pursued.

◇ Other qualifications—hobbies, organizations you belong to, honors you have received, and leadership positions you have held.

◇ Office machines, tools, and equipment you have used, and skills that you possess.

Other information, such as your Social Security number, is often asked for on application forms but is rarely presented on resumes. Application forms might also ask for a record of past addresses and for information that you would rather not reveal, such as a record of convictions. If asked for such information, you must be honest. Honesty does not, however, require that you reveal disabilities that do not affect your overall qualifications for a job. It is also not legal for an employer to ask your age, sex, marital status, race, or religious denomination on an application.

Know thy job

Next, gather specific information about the jobs you are applying for. You need to know the pay range (so you can make their top your bottom), education and experience usually required, hours and shifts usually worked. Most importantly, you need to know the job duties (so that you can describe your experience in terms of those duties). Study the job description. Some job announcements, especially those issued by a government, even have a checklist that assigns a numerical weight to different qualifications so that you can be certain as to which is the most important. Looking at such announcements will give you an idea of what employers look for, even if you do not wish to apply for a government job. If the announcement or ad is vague, call the employer to learn what is sought.

Once you have the information you need, you can prepare a resume. You may need to prepare more than one master resume if you are going to look for different kinds of jobs. Otherwise, your resume will not fit all the jobs you seek.

Two kinds of resumes

The way you arrange your resume depends on how well your experience seems to prepare you for the position you want. Basically, you can either describe your most recent job first and work backwards (reverse chronology) or group similar skills together. No matter which format you use, the following advice applies generally.

◇ Use specifics. A vague description of your duties will make only a vague impression.

◇ Identify accomplishments. If you headed a project, improved productivity, reduced costs, increased membership, or achieved some other goal, say so.

◇ Type your resume, using a standard typeface. (Printed resumes are becoming more common, but employers do not indicate a preference for them.)

◇ Keep the length down to two pages at the most.

◇ Remember your mother's advice not to say anything if you cannot say something nice. Leave all embarrassing or negative information off the resume—but be ready to deal with it in a positive fashion at the interview.

◇ Proofread the master copy carefully.

◇ Have someone else proofread the master copy carefully.

◇ Have a third person proofread the master copy carefully.

◇ Use the best quality photocopying machine and good white or off-white paper.

The following information appears on almost every resume.

◇ Name.

◇ Phone number at which you can be reached or receive messages.

◇ Address.

◇ Job or career sought.

◇ References—often just a statement that references are available suffices. If your references are likely to be known by the person who reads the resume, however, their names are worth listing.

◇ Experience.

◇ Education.

◇ Special talents.

◇ Personal information—height, weight, marital status, physical condition. Although this information appears on virtually every sample resume I have ever seen, it is not important according to recruiters. In fact, employers are prohibited by law from asking for some of it. If some of this information is directly job related—the height and weight of a bouncer is important to a disco owner, for example—list it. Otherwise, save space and put in more information about your skills.

Reverse chronology is the easiest method to use. It is also the least effective because it makes when you did something more important than what you can do. It is an especially poor format if you have gaps in your work history, if the job you seek is very different from the job you currently hold, or if you are just entering the job market. About the only time you would want to use such a resume is when you have progressed up a clearly defined career ladder and want to move up a rung.

Resumes that are not chronological may be called functional, analytical, skill oriented, creative, or some other name. What is important is that they stress what you can do. The advantage to a potential employer—and, therefore, to your job campaign—should be obvious. The employer can see immediately how you will fit the job. This format also has advantages for many job hunters because it camouflages gaps in paid employment and avoids giving prominence to irrelevant jobs.

You begin writing a functional resume by determining the skills the employer is looking for. Again, study the job description for this information. Next, review your experience and education to see when you demonstrated the ability sought. Then prepare the resume itself, putting first the information that relates most obviously to the job. The result will be a resume with headings such as "Engineering," "Computer Languages," "Communications Skills," or "Design Experience." These headings will have much more impact than the dates that you would use on a chronological resume.

Fit yourself to a form

Some large employers, such as fast food restaurants and government agencies, make more use of application forms than of resumes. The forms suit the style of large organizations because people find information more quickly if it always appears in the same place. However, creating a resume before filling out an application form will still benefit you. You can use the resume when you send a letter inquiring about a position. You can submit a resume even if an application is required; it will spotlight your qualifications. And the information on the resume will serve as a handy reference if you must fill out an application form quickly. Application forms are really just resumes in disguise anyway. No matter how rigid the form appears to be, you can still use it to show why you are the person for the job.

At first glance, application forms seem to give a job hunter no leeway. The forms certainly do not have the flexibility that a resume does, but you can still use them to your best advantage. Remember that the attitude of the person reading the form is not, "Let's find out why this person is unqualified," but, "Maybe this is the person we want." Use all the parts of the form—experience blocks, education blocks, and others—to show that the person is you.

Here's some general advice on completing application forms.

◇ Request two copies of the form. If only one is provided, photocopy it before you make a mark on it. You'll need more than one copy to prepare rough drafts.

◇ Read the whole form before you start completing it.

◇ Prepare a master copy if the same form is used by several divisions within the same company or organization. Do not put the specific job applied for, the date, or your signature on the master copy. Fill in that information on the photocopies as you submit them.

◇ Type the form if possible. If it has lots of little lines that are hard to type within, type the information on a piece of blank paper that will fit in the space, paste the paper over the form, and photocopy the finished product. Such a procedure results in a much neater, easier to read page.

◇ Leave no blanks; enter n/a (for "not applicable") when the information requested does not apply to you; this tells people checking the form that you did not simply skip the question.

◇ Carry a resume and a copy of other frequently asked information (such as previous addresses) with you when visiting potential employers in case you must fill out an application on the spot. Whenever possible, however, fill the form out at home and mail it in with a resume and cover letter that point up your strengths.

Writing Intriguing Cover Letters

You will need a cover letter whenever you send a resume or application form to a potential employer. The letter should capture the employer's attention, show why you are writing, indicate why your employment will benefit the company, and ask for an interview. The kind of specific information that must be included in a letter means that each must be written individually. Each letter must also be typed perfectly, which may present a problem. Word processing equipment helps. Frequently only the address, first paragraph, and specifics concerning an interview will vary. These items are easily changed on word processing equipment and memory typewriters. If you do not have access to such equipment, you might be able to rent it. Or you might be able to have your letters typed by a resume or employment services company listed in the yellow pages. Be sure you know the full cost of such a service before agreeing to use one.

Let's go through a letter point by point.

Salutation

Each letter should be addressed by name to the person you want to talk with. That person is the one who can hire you. This is almost certainly not someone in the personnel department, and it is probably not a department head either. It is most likely to be the person who will actually supervise you once you start work. Call the company to make sure you have the right name. And spell it correctly.

Opening

The opening should appeal to the reader. Cover letters are sales letters. Sales are made after you capture a person's attention. You capture the reader's attention most easily by talking about the company rather than yourself. Mention projects under development, recent awards, or favorable comments recently published about the company. You can find such information in the business press, including the business section of local newspapers and the many magazines that are devoted to particular industries. If you are answering an ad, you may mention it. If someone suggested that you write, use their name (with permission, of course).

Body

The body of the letter gives a brief description of your qualifications and refers to the resume, where your sales campaign can continue.

Closing

You cannot have what you do not ask for. At th. end of the letter, request an interview. Suggest a time and state that you will confirm the appointment. Use a standard complimentary close, such as "Sincerely yours," leave three or four lines for your signature, and type your name. You might type your phone number under your name; this recommendation is not usually made, although phone numbers are found on most letterheads. The alternative is to place the phone number in the body of the letter, but it will be more difficult to find there should the reader wish to call you.

Triumphing on Tests and at Interviews

A man with a violin case stood on a subway platform in The Bronx. He asked a train conductor, "How do you get to Carnegie Hall?" The conductor replied, "Practice! Practice! Practice!"

Tests

That old joke holds good advice for people preparing for employment tests or interviews. The tests given to job applicants fall into four categories: General aptitude tests, practical tests, tests of physical agility, and medical examinations. You can practice for the first three. If the fourth is required, learn as soon as possible what the disqualifying conditions are, then have your physician examine you for them so that you do not spend years training for a job that you will not be allowed to hold.

To practice for a test, you must learn what the test is. Once again, you must know what job you want to apply for and for whom you want to work in order to find out what tests, if any, are required. Government agencies, which frequently rely on tests, will often provide a sample of the test they use. These samples can be helpful even if an employer uses a different test. Copies of standard government tests are usually available at the library.

If you practice beforehand, you'll be better prepared and less nervous on the day of the test. That will put you ahead of the competition. You will also improve your performance by following this advice:

◇ Make a list of what you will need at the test center, including a pencil; check it before leaving the house.

◇ Get a good night's sleep.

◇ Be at the test center early—at least 15 minutes early.

◇ Read the instructions carefully; make sure they do not differ from the samples you practiced with.

◇ Generally, speed counts; do not linger over difficult questions.

◇ Learn if guessing is penalized. Most tests are scored by counting up the right answers; guessing is all to the good. Some tests are scored by counting the right answers and deducting partial credit for wrong answers; blind guessing will lose you points—but if you can eliminate two wrong choices, a guess might still pay off.

Interviews

For many of us, interviews are the most fearsome part of finding a job. But they are also our best chance to show an employer our qualifications. Interviews are far more flexible than application forms or tests. Use that flexibility to your advantage. As with tests, you can reduce your anxiety and improve your performance by preparing for your interviews ahead of time.

Begin by considering what interviewers want to know. You represent a risk to the employer. A hiring mistake is expensive in terms of lost productivity, wasted training money, and the cost of finding a replacement. To lessen the risk, interviewers try to select people who are highly motivated, understand what the job entails, and show that their background has prepared them for it.

You show that you are highly motivated by learning about the company before the interview, by dressing appropriately, and by being well mannered—which means that you greet the interviewer by name, you do not chew gum or smoke, you listen attentively, and you thank the interviewer at the end of the session. You also show motivation by expressing interest in the job at the end of the interview.

You show that you understand what the job entails and that you can perform it when you explain how your qualifications prepare you for specific duties as described in the company's job listing and when you ask intelligent questions about the nature of the work and the training provided new workers.

One of the best ways to prepare for an interview is to have some practice sessions with a friend or two. Here is a list of some of the most commonly asked questions to get you started.

◇ Why did you apply for this job?

◇ What do you know about this job or company?

◇ Why should I hire you?

◇ What would you do if. . . (usually filled in with a work-related crisis)?

◇ How would you describe yourself?

◇ What would you like to tell me about yourself?

◇ What are your major strengths?

◇ What are your major weaknesses?

◇ What type of work do you like to do best?

◇ What are your interests outside work?

◇ What type of work do you like to do least?

◇ What accomplishment has given you the greatest satisfaction?

◇ What was your worst mistake?

◇ What would you change in your past life?

◇ What courses did you like best or least in school?

◇ What did you like best or least about your last job?

◇ Why did you leave your last job?

◇ Why were you fired?

◇ How does your education or experience relate to this job?

◇ What are your goals?

◇ How do you plan to reach them?

◇ What do you hope to be doing in 5 years? 10?

◇ What salary do you expect?

Many jobhunting books available at libraries discuss ways to answer these questions. Essentially, your strategy should be to concentrate on the job and your ability to do it no matter what the question seems to be asking. If asked for a strength, mention something job related. If asked for a weakness, mention a job-related strength (you work too hard, you worry too much about details, you always have to see the big picture). If asked about a disability or a specific negative factor in your past—a criminal record, a failure in school, being fired—be prepared to stress what you learned from the experience, how you have overcome the shortcoming, and how you are now in a position to do a better job.

So far, only the interviewer's questions have been discussed. But an interview will be a two-way conversation. You really do need to learn more about the position to find out if you want the job. Given how frustrating it is to look for a job, you do not want to take just any position only to learn after two weeks that you cannot stand the place and have to look for another job right away. Here are some questions for you to ask the interviewer.

◇ What would a day on this job be like?

◇ Whom would I report to? May I meet this person?

◇ Would I supervise anyone? May I meet them?

◇ How important is this job to the company?

◇ What training programs are offered?

◊ What advancement opportunities are offered?

◊ Why did the last person leave this job?

◊ What is that person doing now?

◊ What is the greatest challenge of this position?

◊ What plans does the company have with regard to . . . ? (Mention some development about which you have read or heard.)

◊ Is the company growing?

After you ask such questions, listen to the interviewer's answers and then, if at all possible, point to something in your education or experience related to it. You might notice that questions about salary and fringe benefits are not included in the above list. Your focus at a first interview should be the company and what you will do for it, not what it will pay you. The salary range will often be given in the ad or position announcement, and information on the usual fringe benefits will be available from the personnel department. Once you have been offered a position, you can negotiate the salary. The jobhunting guides available in bookstores and at the library give many more hints on this subject.

At the end of the interview, you should know what the next step will be: Whether you should contact the interviewer again, whether you should provide more information, whether more interviews must be conducted, and when a final decision will be reached. Try to end on a positive note by reaffirming your interest in the position and pointing out why you will be a good choice to fill it.

Immediately after the interview, make notes of what went well and what you would like to improve. To show your interest in the position, send a follow-up letter to the interviewer, providing further information on some point raised in the interview and thanking the interviewer once again. Remember, someone is going to hire you; it might be the person you just talked to.